LANGUAGE LIVE!

KEY STAGE 3

John Seely

HEINEMANN
EDUCATIONAL

Contents

National Curriculum Levels and Strands

Speaking & Listening	Reading	Writing	Presentation
7d, 10e	10e		
7d, 10e			
7d			
7d			
7d		6a, 7a, 8c	
5d, 7b, 7d, 8b		5e	
	7c		6d, 7d
	5e, 6b	5a, 5e, 6a, 7a	
			6d, 7d
	5e, 6b, 7b	5a, 5e, 6a, 7a, 7c, 7e	
			5b, 6b, 7b
6d, 7d			
10e			
		5c, 5e	
		5e	
		6e	
		5c, 5e	
		5c, 5e, 6e	
5b, 6a, 7c		5a, 5c, 6a	
		5a, 5c, 5d, 6a, 6b, 7a, 7b	
	6e, 8e		
			7a
			7a
		5b, 5e, 6b, 7b, 8b	
	5b, 5e, 6b, 7a, 7b, 8a, 8b		
5e, 6e			
5e, 6e, 8e			
5e			

Language Live ! Key stage 3 is the second of a series of three books focusing on knowledge about language for the National Curriculum. It develops the concepts about language introduced in the *Foundation* book in a more detailed and systematic way, providing thorough coverage of relevant statements of attainment and programmes of study for this key stage.

The main chapters of the book focus on specific language themes which form parts of the programmes of study for knowledge about language in the National Curriculum. Each theme is explored in a number of different ways. Sometimes an individual spread provides a discrete unit of work. At others it is necessary to follow through two, three or more spreads to cover a topic fully. Grammatical topics are integrated into the other work, as recommended by the National Curriculum.

A feature of this book, which does not appear in the *Foundation* book is a series of projects: *The magazine, Community Service Volunteers, Words in action.* Each of these offers opportunities for integrated work on a number of the language themes which are the subjects of individual chapters.

Using the cassette

The audio cassette is an integral part of these learning materials. The occasions when its use is recommended are indicated by this symbol.

In almost every instance a transcript of the words spoken appears in this book. It is therefore open to teachers and classes to listen to the cassette with or without the printed text. At some point, however, it will normally be desirable to follow the transcript while listening to the speech.

A number of the recordings made for the introductory unit 'Talking about language' are used again later in the book, in those chapters where the language points raised are considered more fully. They are combined in different ways. In order to avoid confusion and save time, this material occurs again on the cassette in the relevant place.

Contents

For items marked * the cassette provides extended dialogue which is not transcribed in the book.

TALKING ABOUT LANGUAGE

This book is about language, how we use it, and the different ways in which it affects our lives. When we were preparing it we interviewed a number of ordinary people and asked them their opinions about English and the way in which it is used today. This chapter contains some of the things they said. All the comments are on the cassette and as you listen to them you will get an introduction to some of the themes of this book.

Many of the comments appear again, in later chapters that deal in much more detail with the points they raise. When you have worked on those chapters you should be able to comment on what the speakers say in a more thorough and informed way.

You expect 'em to speak English

A Every country uses English its used nationally in aircraft in ships

B If we go abroad on holiday you expect em to speak English you havent got any trouble in making yourself clear I mean you just go into a restaurant and theyll speak English as well as you

A I think English is a world language and absorbs words from every other country so youve got a vocabulary in English its got millions of words in it

B Ive often thought to myself well now England has been invaded by various countries the Romans and and French and so forth now I cant erm understand why we don't talk Italian how did the English language get formulated thats puzzled me England little tiny country gainst all the world and everybody wants to learn English

---

What do you think ?

1 Discuss with other people your experience of meeting people from other European countries. Did you find that you could make yourself understood in English ?

2 How well did the people you met speak English ?

3 Why do so many people throughout the world want to speak English ?

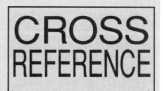

CROSS REFERENCE

Page 56

VERY SLAPHAPPY

C I think its very slaphappy spoken English today

D It has changed for the worse it grates on us elder people the way our lovely English language has been disregarded I mean Ive got twenty-five grandchildren its a different way of teaching theyve got today havent they we were taught the real old-fashioned way to pronounce our vowels and verbs and proverbs and all the rest of it if we didnt do it we got chastised we had to speak clearly or else we were told to sit down

B If you dont speak clearly and erm pronounce your words proply then thats bad English I I think thats why you go to college to learn to speak you know the first class English but if you go to an ordinary school well anything could happen you could learn English but you wont pronounce it quite so thoroughly as what a a a student in a college would do

E If you want to hear the finest English spoken English go to Invernessshire the pronounciation (sic) of words is fantastic its clear theyll tell you up there they speak the finest English and they do

F Possibly the rush of daily life means that people dont have time to relish and enjoy the use of words for themselves there is perhaps a a less rich turn of phrase when I sit down with rural people sometimes Im delighted by the poetic and concrete imagery that these people use and I I realize that erm being in an urban environment means sometimes that my own language becomes excessively abstract and a bore

G Hospitalization for instance the American way of speaking I think thats all wrong well hospitalization there's never such a word was there am I right or am I wrong and all those -izations Americans are always doing that arent they and of course a lot of swearing terrible amount of swearing going on I wont repeat because I dont swear much myself

H Dont really notice it until you like go somewhere with like your mum cos my mum really doesnt like swearing I went shopping with her and we were sitting on the bus and there were these all these guys sitting at the back and just literally every other word was a swear word I mean they were having a conversation and you know they were boasting about their weekend and what they were going to do and everything and just every other word was a swear word and it was beginning to make me cringe cos I knew that my mum she was like getting annoyed about the swear words and that was making me feel uncomfortable and I knew that she was going to say something and I was like going to have to stand next to this woman on the bus who was going to say like will you just shut up and it doesnt mean anything anyway

F I don't mind erm the swear words but when people use cliches I think the kind of language I most object to are erm DJ patter and and some some sports commentary is is so erm so much fill that it becomes actually funny Id much rather have an announcer say we will now have two minutes of silence until the next event some of our nature documentaries I think have really set a new standard of only saying something when theres something to be said and allowing the image to speak for itself

What do you think ?

1 Some older people think that language has changed for the worse. What do you think they mean by 'good' and 'bad' when talking about language. Do you agree with them ?

2 What do you think about swearing ? Why do people do it ? Why are some words called 'swear words' ? Why are people shocked or hurt by them ?

3 What makes you irritated or angry about language and the way people use it ?

CROSS REFERENCES

Page 56
Pages 12-13
Page 32

J Because I was bullied quite a lot in middle school I made a conscious effort to change the way I spoke like when when its getting a bit violent in the pub or something and the group's picking on one particular person the person thats being picked on will automatically adopt an accent which is quite close to the one thats threatening them or if theyre trying to impress someone the same thing the accent changes

F I myself am aware that erm when Im with strangers my accent tends to become more nearly British because Im trying to be accepted and Im trying to reduce the blocks to communication as much as I can but if I get excited or if Im amongst friends I my American comes out and its quite embarrassing to me and in fact my children have pointed out that I tend to speak pidgin with foreigners and go all English with English people and erm you see I have no linguistic integrity at all totally a chameleon

J I spent three weeks in America last summer and by the time I got back I was told that the way I spoke was actually quite different the Americans were were noticing that I had an American accent and the English noticed that my sentences went up at the end instead of down like if you say dyou wed say do you want a cup of tea and itd go down with the tea at the end but if like when when Catherine speaks or when the Americans speak its like dyou want a cup of tea

K So dyou want a cup of tea eh yeah I do add eh to the end of sentences that is a common trait of all New Zealanders I didnt realise I was doing it until I came here

I People from Yorkshire or even when I was in Birmingham people from the Black Country they have a definite way of speaking with themselves or in their family it wont be as particular

L This here is a slightly formal situation and youre ticking over at a different rate youre not exactly relaxed youre being very careful about the way youre speaking the words youre going to use had we been doing this in a pub after a couple of pints we may well have been talking in a different manner you know youd be more excitable more relaxed and less conscious use of the words that youre putting together to form your sentences youd be saying anything anyhow

K I think everyone adapts to their situation though when theyre with friends they definitely talk in a more flippant erm relaxed laid back manner than they would if they were talking to parents or the Principal or teachers or something like that

M If I was talking to an older who I respected I would pronounce the words right but if I was just talking to a mate of mine Id just slur and itd just be sort of like a different language

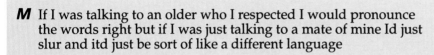

J You go like anyfing and not anything but when you come over to my house and talk to my parents its everythings just that little bit more correct grammatically like you wont miss out your Ts when you talk to them and you go anything and not anyfing but thats thats not you to change that

K I know that my brother grunts when he communicates erm the school that he was at in New Zealand all of his friends it was like a very academic school but all of his friends seemed to manage to communicate with each other by just sort of talking like this you know they just sort of like you know throw everything together and I could never understand what they were talking about because they just you know it was you know a sort of male sort of thing to do was to sort of talk like this all the time it was really ridiculous because they were intelligent young men and yet they seemed to er ----everything----come ---- out ---- and Id be going out with someone from the same school and they had exactly the same thing I just had to keep saying can you tell me what youre trying to say cos I didnt understand it was like this necessity to just grunt and and squash everything up together

M Like we say oh yeah n that but it doesnt mean anything you just say it if someone taps you on the shoulder you go oh yeah n that and sort of like it means nothing but yet they know what you mean

What do you think ?

1 Many of these speakers believe that people judge them by the way they speak. Do you judge people by how they speak ?

2 Do you think other people judge you in this way ?

3 Is it right to do that ?

4 They also believe that people change the way they speak according to the company they are in. Is this true in your experience ?

CROSS REFERENCES

Page 33
Pages 10-11

Topic, audience, format, purpose

How well we communicate depends on how carefully we pay attention to four questions:

- What am I talking about?
- Who am I trying to communicate with?
- Why am I trying to communicate with them?
- How should I shape what I want to say?

Adapting

J Because I was bullied quite a lot in middle school I made a conscious effort to change the way I spoke. Like when it's getting a bit violent in the pub or something and the group's picking on one particular person: the person that's being picked on will automatically adopt an accent which is quite close to the one that's threatening them. Or if they're trying to impress someone, the same thing: the accent changes.

K I think everyone adapts to their situation, though. When they're with friends they definitely talk in a more flippant, relaxed, laid back manner than they would if they were talking to parents or the Principal or teachers or something like that.

Personal research

Think about where you have been, what you have done and what you have said during the last two hours. Make a list of the main people you have spoken to during that time. Against each one write brief answers to these questions:

1 What kind of thing did you talk about?

2 How well would you say you know that person/those people?

3 How would you describe the way you spoke to them? (eg Polite/relaxed/angry...)

Comment and discussion

1 Do you agree with what Speaker K says about adapting?

2 Can you think of examples where you might behave in the way described by Speaker J?

HOME AND AWAY

M

If I was talking to an older who I respected, I would pronounce the words right, but if I was just talking to a mate of mine I'd just slur and it'd just be sort of like a different language.

J

You go like 'Anyfing' and not 'Anything' but when you come over to my house and talk to my parents it's... everything's just that little bit more correct grammatically. Like you won't miss out your Ts when you talk to them, and you go 'Anything' and not 'Anyfing' but that's not you to change that.

Discussion points

1 She says, 'that's not you to change that.' So why does he do it ?

2 Do you think he is being insincere to behave like this ?

3 Do you know people who change their speech like this ?

4 Do you ?

5 Is it a good thing to do ?

THE CASE OF THE GRUNTING SCHOOLBOYS

K

I know that my brother grunts when he communicates. The school that he was at in New Zealand - all of his friends - it was like a very academic school. But all of his friends seemed to manage to communicate with each other by just sort of talking like this (mimics) you know - they just sort of like - you know - throw everything together... And I could never understand what they were talking about, because they just -(mimics again) you know - it was - you know a sort of male sort of thing to do was to sort of talk like this all the time... It was really ridiculous because they were intelligent young men and yet they seemed to (mimics again) er ----everything ----come ---- out ----
And I'd be going out with someone from the same school and they had exactly the same thing. I just had to keep saying, 'Can you tell me what you're trying to say ?' 'cos I didn't understand. It was like this necessity to just grunt and and squash everything up together.

M

Like we say, 'Oh yeah 'n' that,' but it doesn't mean anything. You just say it. If someone taps you on the shoulder you go, 'Oh yeah 'n' that,' and sort of like it means nothing but yet they know what you mean.

1 Why do you think the boys behaved in the way described by Speaker K ?

2 Have you ever come across people who act in this way ?

3 What do you think Speaker M means by 'Oh yeah 'n' that' ?

4 Can you think of other expressions like that ?

5 If so, what are they and what do people mean by them ?

¡Language!

G

...and of course a lot of swearing - terrible amount of swearing going on. I won't repeat, because I dont swear much myself.

H

Don't really notice it until you go somewhere with, like, your mum - 'cos my mum really doesn't like swearing. I went shopping with her, and we were sitting on the bus, and there were these all these guys sitting at the back and just literally every other word was a swear word. I mean they were having a conversation and - you know - they were boasting about their weekend and what they were going to do and everything. And just every other word was a swear word and it was beginning to make me cringe, 'cos I knew that my mum she was, like, getting annoyed about the swear words. And that was making me feel uncomfortable and I knew that she was going to say something and I was going to have to, like, stand next to this woman on the bus who was going to say, like, 'Will you just shut up !' And it doesn't mean anything anyway.

1. Why is it that some words are considered bad ?
2. Is there something about swear words that makes them different from other words ?
3. Are there occasions when it is 'all right to swear' ?

Role play

Imagine that the girl's mother does speak to the people on the bus who are swearing. The girl is embarrassed. When they get home they talk about it. Role play their conversation.

F I don't mind the swear words but when people use cliches... I think the kind of language I most object to are DJ patter... and some some sports commentary is so much 'fill' that it becomes actually funny. I'd much rather have an announcer say, 'We will now have two minutes of silence until the next event.' Some of our nature documentaries I think have really set a new standard of only saying something when there's something to be said and allowing the image to speak for itself.

The word is that our new logo is a real stunner. Kenton's just come back from having seen a preview of Radio 1's new promo and he reckons it's just Mmmmmmm ! Why haven't I seen it ? No one asked my approval of anything. Just disgraceful.

Radio 1 DJ Mike is another year older today. Probably and hopefully taking out Jakki Brambles tonight. He'll be picking her up from Top of the Pops, swinging her away for a wild evening, and then getting her home and in bed by ten o'clock. Then he'll go to his own home before you start thinking like that. Jakki Brambles' birthday today; it's also Mike Reid's birthday...

Simon Bates : BBC Radio 1 1/3/90

Well it's Ipswich 0, Liverpool 2, and if that's the way the score stays then you've got to fancy Liverpool to win.

1 Do you agree with her about 'DJ patter' ?

2 Can you think of any reasons why DJs should talk at length about nothing very much ?

3 Do you think she is right that TV sports commentators should simply say far less ?

4 Can you think of other examples when people just say far too much about very little ?

5 What do you think she means by the word cliche ? Can you think of examples ?

Topic...

For every topic there is a range of words we can use: the vocabulary that is suitable for that topic.

SPECIALIST TERMS

Some subjects require the use of specialist terms: words which apply only to that topic, or to a small range of related topics. For example:

A

To open it you only need to put down £1 - although of course we'll accept more. Then you can watch the interest grow and grow. The more your savings grow, the higher the rate of interest. And whenever you want to withdraw cash you can - with no penalties !

B

...3- or 5-door versions with head-restraints, rear wash/wipe, tinted windows and central locking all as standard...

C

...then pull the weft tight, so that the warp threads will be drawn in. This reduces the width of the braid to about half what you started with. Don't worry about the sett of the warp, either, because in this method....

D

...tickets can be obtained at the station, or from a large number of travel agents. Once on the platform you will find facilities compare very favourably with those in Britain. There is usually a small buffet, as well as the usual waiting-rooms and so on.
Once your journey has begun you will find that the facilities on board are also good. Most carriages are open plan and air-conditioned. Reclining seats are common and if you are prepared to spend a little more you can travel in one of the delightful observation cars...

E

Another problem you may come up against is fret buzz. If this happens, the thing to do is to try to work out the reasons. It may be that the action is too low (ie less than 1.5mm on the bass side and 1 mm on the treble). Another cause could be uneven fret height. This could be the result of a crown in the neck or a forward bow. Try holding the top E string down at the last fret and...

F

...using a zoom lens. Of course, in low-light you will find it difficult, because the widest aperture of such a lens is often only 5.6. This gives you a choice of low shutter speeds or a very small depth of field...

For each text, answer these questions:

1 What is the topic ?
2 What are the specialist words ?
3 Which of the words in the list opposite belongs to the topic ?

bumper	focus	plectrum
chord	invest	spoiler
deposit	loom	terminus
filter	luggage	weave

...and audience

How we combine words into sentences depends not only on the topic, but also on our audience.

> Pull the end of the film across the back. See those little holes in the side ? Line them up with the teeth in the wheel...

> ... then you pull the film leader across behind the shutter curtain until the perforations are aligned with the sprocket teeth ...

Both these speakers are explaining the same thing, but they are using different vocabulary and different kinds of sentence.

1 What are the differences in the words used ?
2 How do the patterns of the sentences differ ?
3 Why are there these differences ?

Writing

1 Choose a topic that you are familiar with - or take one from this list :

football	chemistry	fashion
computers	biology	tennis

2 Make a list of special words relating to that topic.

3 You are going to write two explanations about some aspect of your chosen topic:
(a) for someone who already knows something about it;
(b) for a child of 9, who has just become interested in it.
Decide what aspect you will write about and which of the words on your list you could use with each audience.

4 Now write your explanation for audience (a).

5 Read through what you have written and think about the needs of audience (b). What will you have to do to help that person understand ?

6 Now write your explanation for audience (b).

software
computer
keyboard
VDU screen
programme
floppy disk
hard disk
byte
megabyte
printer
operating system
cursor

chine that can be
or many different
es. You can use it
do sums, to type
ters and stories to
d organise all sorts
of information. Computers
can also be used to run
large machines in factories
and to control the central
heating in buildings

At the travel agency

The assistant's job

You are the assistant at the travel agency. You have to :
- discuss the choice of hotels with your customers
- help them fill in the application form

1 Would you tackle this in exactly the same way with each customer ? If not, how would your approach differ ?

2 What would be the most difficult part of your job, do you think ? How could you make it easier ?

Role play

Pairs : the assistant and one of the customers.

1 Decide which customer and who plays each part.

2 Think about your role and how you will approach the conversation:
Assistant - remember how you decided you would speak to this customer.
Customer - decide what kind of person you are and how you will speak to the assistant.

3 When you are both ready start the conversation.

4 After each conversation talk about these discussion points:

a) Did people change their language according to their audience ?

b) If so, in what ways did they change ?

c) Was their language suitable for their audience ?

d) If not, how could it have been improved ?

APPLICATION FORM

Surname _____   **Forenames** _____

Address _____   **Telephone number** _____

_____   **Passport number** ☐☐☐☐☐☐☐☐

1	**2**	**3**
Country Resort Hotel	Country Resort Hotel	Country Resort Hotel

Hotel Bristol

We think : *Just the choice for a lively family holiday with lots to do all the time. Not suitable for anyone who has problems with steps.*

The Bristol is one of the biggest hotels on this part of the coast, and certainly the liveliest, with a full range of recreation and entertainment facilities for adults and children:

- huge swimming pool with bar terrace
- large lounge bar
- Happy Hour every evening
- three tennis courts, trampolines, table tennis, crazy golf
- complete children's playground including pool

Hotel Cola Pineda

We think : *Slap bang in the middle of town, the Cola Pineda is just right for lively people who want to be in the thick of things.*

This hotel is situated in the centre of town, only a few minutes' walk from the promenade and beach. In the town centre - busy and bustling - is everything you could ask for in the way of shops, bars, restaurants and discos, but the hotel has plenty to offer, too:

- swimming pool with terrace and bar
- large lounge bar
- twenties bar with pool table
- video room
- music till late !

Hotel del Ingles

We think : *a friendly restful hotel for those who want a complete break.*

The Hotel del Ingles is placed in a quiet backwater away from the traffic noise and bustle of the town centre, yet only a short walk from a pleasant and secluded beach. It offers old-style service at a price that is very reasonable:

- small pool with attached sun lounge
- air-conditioned dining room with full waiter service
- quiet lounge with separate bar

ormat

Texts communicate through words and sentences, of course. But they also communicate through the way in which those words and sentences are set out on the page. We call this the format of the text.

Examples

For each of these examples, explain what the text is about and how you think the format suits that text.

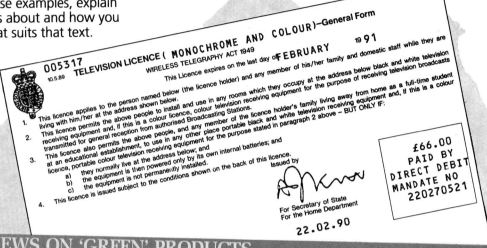

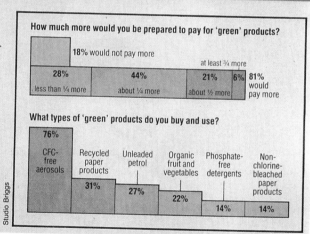

YOUR VIEWS ON 'GREEN' PRODUCTS

Last March we carried out a survey of 2,450 *Which?* members, to find out their views on buying 'green' products.
● Nearly 90% said they think about the environmental effects of products when they buy and use them, at least some of the time.
● About 80% said they'd be prepared to pay extra for products which are less harmful to the environment. Of these, 28% would pay less than a quarter as much again, 44% would pay about a quarter as much again, 21% would pay about half as much again, and 6% would pay three-quarters or more of the price again.
● CFC-free aerosols were the most commonly-bought 'green' product; of members who considered the environment when shopping, 76% buy these. Next came recycled paper and paper products (31%), unleaded petrol (27%), organic fruit and vegetables (22%), phosphate-free detergents (14%), and paper products which aren't chlorine-bleached (14%).
● But while members were keen to buy products which are less harmful to the environment, 88% of them thought that shops were not doing enough to promote such products.

Studio Briggs

Features

Format includes these features:
- printing or writing
- the kind of print used (the typeface, or font)
- the sizes of print or writing used
- the size of the paper and the size of the text on it
- the use of illustrations
- the way the text is arranged on the page

When we see a particular format, we expect the text to be written in a particular way to suit that format. In fact, as soon as we see a particular format, we expect a particular kind of text.

What's wrong ?

On the facing page there are five texts and five formats. The trouble is that the texts have been presented in the wrong formats. Which text should go with which format ? Use a table like this to help you work it out.

Number	Kind of text	Kind of format
1	Personal letter	tabloid newspaper

1

I CAN'T TELL YOU
HOW MUCH I ENJOYED THE TRIP TO SEE 'INDIANA JONES' !

And of course being with you again made the occasion something else again ! Do you remember the first time we saw a film together ? It was early last summer and we'd been planning to go boating on the river. Then the heavens opened and we were stuck in the middle of Oxford with nothing to do.

2

OOPS !
TV megastar Crocker Twite has done it again. Right in front of the Queen ! At yesterday's Royal Garden Party in the grounds of Buckingham Palace he shocked the rich and the famous by his behaviour. Just as the Queen was passing, he

3

Jones, A, 23 Ronson Street Carmarthen 2308 Jones, A, The Gahir, Cwmsyr Chirk 20193 Jones, A, 49 Penton Lane Ross-on-Wye 89775 Jones, A, 21 Staunton Clo Hereford 284745

4

Ford Fiesta 1988
silver
Only one owner
27600 miles

V.G.C.   *2100 o.n.o.*

5

Shall I compare thee.....................................to a summer's day ?	**By** chance, or natures.....................
Thou art more lovely...........................and more temperate:	**But** thy eternall............................
Rough winds do shake.........................the darling buds of May	**Nor** lose possession.......................
And summer's sun................................hath all too short a date:	**Nor** shall death...........................
Sometime too hot............................. the eye of heaven shines,	**When** in eternall...........................
And often is his................................ gold complexion dimm'd	**So** long as men...........................
And every faire.......................:..... from faire some–time declines,	**So** long lives this...........................

All the texts on this page and the next two are about Morocco, so they have a similar subject matter, but the writers' purposes are very different. As you read each one, and look at any illustrations that accompany it, ask yourself, 'What is the writer's purpose in this text ?'

Shot on location in Tangier, Agadir and Marrakech.

EVERYTHING YOU'D EXPECT.

MOROCCO

MORE THAN YOU'D DREAM.

From the minute you set foot in Morocco you're treated like a star.

With the finest food, the most luxurious hotels and a perfect climate taking care of all your creature comforts.

But whether you've come for the beaches and year-round sun of Agadir, or the twin Mediterranean and Atlantic shores of Tangier, you'll find that sitting back and soaking up the sun and ambience is far from the whole story.

For in places like Marrakech, or any of the Imperial cities, you are on location in some of the most exciting settings in the world.

Where spectacle, mystery, romance and history lie around every corner.

Places where every sense is stimulated and you are the heroes of the adventure of a lifetime.

And free to write your own script.

For all the sights, sensations and characters are there just waiting to be discovered. And enjoyed, not from the armchair but in vivid, living colour.

Because Morocco is more than just a holiday.

It's a great tale on an epic scale. With a happy ending guaranteed.

For the full story contact your travel agent, send the coupon or phone the Moroccan National Tourist Office, 205 Regent Street, London W1R 7DE. 01-437 0073.

Please send me details of Holidays in Morocco   IM1

Name

Address

Moroccan National Tourist Office, 205 Regent Street, London W1R 7DE

MOROCCO
Tangier

TANGIER

Hotels and Apartments are numbered as follows:
1. Chellah   3. Solazur
2. Rif

Your coach journey from the airport takes approx. 45 mins.

Approx scale in miles

Built up area

THE FRIENDLY CHELLAH IS SET IN ATTRACTIVE GARDENS

OUR OPINION

"A fascinating combination of sun, sea and sand with an intriguing city."

Tangier is a unique and fascinating city. Built on a series of hills overlooking a varied coastline, it's tremendously colourful. There are little squares, handsome tree-lined avenues and residential areas where bougainvillea tumbles over garden walls while TV aerials tangle up above. The vast kasbah boasts 1100 narrow streets, a lovely old Sultan's Palace which is now a museum and innumerable souks where souvenirs can be haggled for. The golden beach is so vast there's plenty of room for all the sunseekers - during the day you can only go on it in swimwear or beachwear (you can leave your other belongings in one of the cabins belonging to the beach bars and restaurants).

HOTEL CHELLAH
テアテ
Tangier

OUR OPINION

"A pleasant, relaxed hotel in a good position for exploring Tangier."

Expect a warm welcome at the Chellah which is a friendly and informal hotel with quite a large lawn and pool at the back even though it's close to the centre of town. It's own beach club is about half a mile away.

➤ swimming pool; sun terrace; garden bar; Beach Club with bar-restaurant, reached by **FREE** hotel bus service
➤ reception lounge with evening bar; daily Happy Hour; lovely air-conditioned Moroccan bar/lounge
➤ dining room; buffet-style breakfast, main courses at dinner waiter service with choice of menu; if clients wish to take lunch, this is served at the beach club; à la carte menu available
➤ **FREE** tennis at the Emsallah Tennis Club; **FREE** table-tennis; darts; daily entertainments

➤ **FREE** afternoon tea; **FREE** Windsurfing at beach club; Reduction on green fees at the Royal Country Golf Club
➤ TV; regular video film shows; shop
➤ dancing most nights to records; weekly Moroccan night available; resident pianist most evenings
➤ playground; early suppers available; **FREE** cots; highchairs available; mini club

Prices: based on half board in a room with two or three beds, with bath and wc.
Supplements: full board; balcony; single room.
Reductions: 3rd adult only in room.

Hotel Bedrooms: 180 • Lifts: 2 • Official Rating: 3A • HotelTel No: 41443

SPECIAL OFFERS

Clients at the Chellah receive:
➤ No single room supp for departures on or after 1/5 returning by 1/6, departures on or after 1/10 returning by 31/10.

THE COSMOPOLITAN TOWN OF TANGIER

Thomson Summer Sun

MOROCCO . Tangier

Midnight Mass

He arrived in Tangier at noon and went straight to the house. In the rain the outer courtyard was uninviting. Several dead banana plants had fallen over and been left to rot on the tile floor. Even as old Amina, seeing him from the kitchen doorway, waddled out in the rain to greet him, he was aware of the piles of empty crates, and of the frame of an ancient garden swing looming behind her.

At lunch he tasted his childhood in Amina's soup. The recipe had not changed; pumpkin and cumin still predominated. All at once he was aware of a cold wind blowing through the room. He called to Amina: the big window in the kitchen was broken. He reminded her that money had been sent to have it repaired. But the wind had come and blown it in again, she said, and this time they had simply left it that way. He told her to shut the door to the kitchen. When she had done it he could not see that it made any difference.

He went through the rooms. The place was only a shell of the house he remembered. Most of the furniture was gone, and there were no rugs or curtains. When he discovered that all six of the fireplaces belched smoke, he had his first doubts about the usefulness of the house as a place to spend the Christmas holidays -at least, that year. It was the only bequest his mother had made him, and she had been reluctant even about that. 'You don't want the house in Tangier. You'll never use it.' 'But I love it,' he objected. 'I grew up in it, after all.' Once she had agreed to leave it to him, she proceeded to strip it of everything of value. A rug went to one friend, a highboy to

7

After being received by Henry's wife I went out almost immediately to call on Paul Bowles, before joining her again later at the Parade bar. I arrived just before the downstairs door was locked. The *assas*, or watchman, of Paul's apartment block, is someone in Tangier totally without my control. Although I 've visited Paul countless times at night over the years, and have lived in the block myself, the *assas* affects absolutely not to recognize me or produce his key until I have first produced a coin. This is upsetting to dignity. I have no objection to tipping (and in Tangier one learns the art with cunning), but to the sequential nature of this particular man's extortion. Charon, Paul calls him. Tonight I've evaded what has long been known between us as the 'Bowles Tax'.

Paul was unchanged: a matchstick man made of mercury, as I think of him; infinitely courteous. With him was the Riffian, Mohammed Mrabet, whose novels and stories he has translated through the oral medium of tapes. I discovered that the flat I had hoped to have reserved had been taken. The confusion was my own fault. I'd been delayed in England longer than intended. Three weeks later I blessed the muddle that prevented my taking what was a small unfurnished flat near my old *haouma* of Aïn Haiani. I'd found an ideal place in the centre of town. It was an exhausting, and often curious, sequence of negotiations which achieved this. But I was determined to long-term rent my own place at last. Meanwhile my temporary hostess was packing up with her small children to return to America. Most of my first week was devoted to helping her.

Sightseeing

Before beginning a detailed sightseeing, a panoramic view from the terrace located at the end of the rue Pasteur permits to embrace all the old city, enclosed in its ramparts, dominated by the kasba and going down till the port and the sea.

The gardens of the ancient Mendoubia, nearby the «Great Socco», also offers, thanks to its milennial dragon-trees, a good place of view on the medina.

From the Great Socco, full of a swarming crowd in coloured clothes, the es Siaghin Street, with its jewellers' shops and where, in 1869, the painter Henri Regnault was living, leads to the little Socco. The famous composer Camile Saint-Saëns dwelled there.

The Marine Street, after going along the Grand Mosque (XVIII th century), leads to a terrace dominating the Borj el Marsa and gives access to Bab el Bahr, the Door of the Sea, in front of the harbour.

From the Great Socco, through the Kasba Street and the Kasba Door, you will have access to the Kasba where, in the Dar el Makhzen (XVIIIth and XIXth centuries), is a museum of Moroccan arts.

Tangiers also offers to the lovers of sports: sea-skiing in the bight, yachting and submarine fishing , golfing, pigeon shooting, tennis, horse-manship.

First response

Make some notes on each of these texts about Morocco. Use these headings, but add any more of your own that you think useful.

  Number
  Description of the text
  The format of the text
  The audience the text is probably aimed at
  How you would describe the purpose of the text
  The points about the language that help you work these things out

Your writing

Now choose a place you know - preferably a holiday place, but it needn't be. Choose three purposes from the notes you have made. Make up texts about your chosen place with the same purpose and for the same audience as each one.

summary

How well we communicate depends on how carefully we pay attention to four questions:

- **What** am I talking about: am I using the right words for this **topic** ?
- **Who** am I trying to communicate with: am I going about it the right way for this **audience** ?
- **How** should I frame my message: what **format** should I use ?
- **Why** am I trying to communicate: what is my **purpose** in communicating ?

ADAPTING

These pages showed you ways in which young people have experienced the need to adapt their speech according to the situation they are in. They altered the way they spoke (their accent and pronunciation); their grammar; and the words and expressions they used.

LANGUAGE !

A special example of the way in which people adapt their language according to the situation is swearing. Some people believe that it is all right to use certain words in certain situations, but they would not dream of using them in other situations, because the words are 'bad'. Other people object to those who seem to be just talking for the sake of it. (Although we all use language without much content sometimes - as a way of getting on with people.) Often when you ask someone, 'How are you ?', you don't really want to know; you just want to make 'friendly noises'.

TOPIC...AND AUDIENCE

Special subjects require special vocabulary, but this may not always be suitable, if the audience is unable to understand it. In such situations the speaker or writer has to find ways of getting round the technical terms in order to explain things clearly.

AUDIENCE

When speaking or writing, we need to be aware of our audience. This awareness includes matters such as age, experience, previous knowledge, and our relationship with them.

FORMAT

Getting the message across is a matter of words and sentences (the grammar of what we say or write). It is also a matter of format: the way in which our words and sentences are shaped. So, for example, the format of a personal letter is very different from that of a newspaper advert. We aren't likely to make mistakes over major differences like that, but the exact format our writing (and speech) takes can be very important.

PURPOSE

Even when topic and audience are the same, speech and writing will vary widely according to our purpose: why do we want to communicate and what effect do we want to have on our audience ?

project: *The magazine*

Introduction

You are the editorial team responsible for the launch of a new magazine. Together you have to
- decide who your magazine is aimed at
- plan the subject matter
- choose a title
- design the cover for the first issue
- plan the page design for the features
- decide which contributions to use and which ones to reject
- edit the material you have selected for publication

Planning your publication

Now it's your turn. Decide these points:
1 What is your target audience ?
2 What are the main kinds of subject matter ?
3 What is the title ?
4 What kind of cover do you want ?

Looking at the covers

The cover is the first thing that people see when looking at magazines in a shop. It has to give clear strong messages about what the magazine is and who it is for. Below are the covers of three magazines. Look at each one carefully and think about the answers to these questions:

1 What is your first impression of the cover as a whole ?
2 What idea does the title give you of (a) the contents of the magazine (b) the audience it is aimed at ?
3 What idea does the illustration give you of (a) the contents of the magazine (b) the audience it is aimed at ?
4 What about the other words on the cover - how do they add to the message given by the title and the illustration ?
5 Which one do you find most attractive and why ?

Making the cover

You should now have enough information to be able to plan your first cover.
1 Try to produce at least two and if possible three or four different rough versions.
2 Discuss these roughs before you decide on the cover you want for your first edition. Then produce a detailed design for it:
   ● use a large sheet of paper so that you can work full-size
   ● mark in the position of your illustration as an outline
   ● put in the title and all the other text as it will appear on the cover
   ● write a description of what the illustration will look like
3 When you have finished you can present your ideas to the rest of the group and discuss their response.

25

Contributions

It is important for an editor to select the type of article the magazine's readers like and expect. This means considering factors such as:

Topic - is this the kind of subject readers will be interested in ?

Treatment - is the writer's approach interesting and lively ?

Tone - does the writer 'talk' to our readers in the right way ? (Or is it too starchy ? or too chatty ?)

Language - is the writing suitable for our readers ? Is it too difficult to understand ? Does it use slang or technical terms they will find difficult or offensive ?

The three extracts below all come from magazine articles about people. Read them carefully and then look at the bottom of page 27.

Daniel and Paul of the new pop duo Yell! are not an entirerly happy pair. They may be storming up the charts with their perky 'debut' single; they may be having a rip-roaring time jigging about with 'Mad Lizzie'; the rubber limbed fitness expert on TVam every morning. But it's not all been fun and games. Because their single is a version of an old song they've been accused of being not much cop at anything except cavorting around the stage and grinning a lot. And they're getting a bit fed up of it.

So-are Yell! really two talentless bimbos or are they, as their publicity claims, 'The New Pop Sensation For The '90's'? Let us examine the facts of the matter...

Yell! are Daniel (aged 22) and Paul (aged 18). Neither of them were much cop at school. Paul ended up working on a building site for a short spell. 'I was just carrying things up ladders on to a roof with no free hands to hold onto the ladder. I couldn't stand it,' he says. Daniel meanwhile worked on a fairground. 'I had this romantic idea of sitting in a caravan and writing some songs. I was doing all sorts of stuff- the dodgems, the waltzers. It was very hard work and very depressing and boring really.'

Both of them had played around in would-be pop groups with tacky names like Hot Ice but all this was really a rehearsal for the partnership that was to become Yell! Daniel was going out with Paul's big sister Joanne and came round one day to meet the family. From the back room of the house he heard a tinkling of keyboards...

'I could hear old twinklefingers here playing in the backroom and I was so impressed...'

'This is going to be an insult, right?'

'I was so impressed, I thought it was Les Dawson.'

Anyway, they both found out they were songwriters and singers, so they decided to form a longterm relationship. Sadly things didn't work out quite so well with Joanne.

'She's, ah...moved on to other things,' explains Daniel, 'so we'd have drifted apart probably anyway.'

Life, eh?

'Maybe I've leaned too much on the clandestine thing,' Al Pacino concedes, a bit ruefully. 'It was a phase I was going through.'

It's a phase he's not entirely out of yet, at least stylistically. Tonight, for instance, he's dressed entirely in black. Black shoes, trousers, shirt, a billowy jacket that looks as if it's been fabricated from black parachute silk.

It suits him. It matches his dark eyes and the dark circles under them. Indeed, the black parachute look is perfectly suited to the role he's played for the last six years: Al Pacino, fugitive movie star, clandestine prince of players, the Hamlet of Hollywood.

Al's 'clandestine thing' can drive Hollywood types crazy, particularly his Hamlet-like indecision about which film projects to commit to, if any.

'Pacino is a schmuck. His career went into the toilet,' an evidently embittered Oliver Stone was quoted in **People** as saying recently - apparently still aggrieved by Pacino's decision (more than 10 years ago) to drop out of **Born on the Fourth of July**.

Hollywood is filled with stories of Oscar-winning roles and films Pacino rejected. And with curiosity over the ones he has actually done such as **Revolution**, the only feature film he made in the six years between **Scarface** in 1983 and his return to the screen in **Sea of Love**.

And so Pacino - arguably the most naturally gifted of the great post-Brando quartet of American actors that includes Hoffman, De Niro and Nicholson - has become a major enigma. What has he been doing in those six years?

Jools Holand is no stranger to the rigours of travelling. Between touring Britain and America with Squeeze and the Jools Holland Big Band, and his various far-flung TV projects, Holland has learned that it's important to make the most of his time spent getting from A to B. 'The main thing about travelling,' he says, 'is that it is incredibly time-consuming. I used to be very fond of looking out the window on a long train journey as a child - happy to just look into people's back gardens, with the odd hope of spotting somebody undressed. But after lots of travelling you find that it's not really satisfying enough to just watch things go past, so I discovered that all that dead time had to be used creatively.'

After a bout with watercolours ('very messy...I was always ending up with a lapful of paint'), Holland has settled on architectural drawing to while away the hours in transit. 'It's far easier. You can't go wrong with a T-square and a little board, really.'

Holland's first major overseas trip was around 1977, on tour with Squeeze. 'I would have been 20, I suppose. It was our first tour of America, and it was all very rough but exciting. I literally had three socks, no change of underpants and a little paper bag with a few belongings in it. The customs people gave me a hard time - they thought I was going to be a vagrant.'

He no longer believes in travelling light, however. 'Now I go away with suitcases and suitcases. And in my hand luggage I always carry the following things: a talking dictionary, a T-square and a pair of binoculars at all times. When you're in the air, you might come across an extraterrestrial or something exciting, like an Iranian plane trying to shoot you down, so it's always handy to try and get a view of it through the binocs and then do a sketch, for the news people.'

What audience ?

What kind of reader do you think each writer was aiming at ? Look at the questions at the top of page 26 and try to decide how they should be answered for each article. You may find it helpful to make up a table like this for each one:

Your writing

Now you try. You know who the readers of your magazine are and what they are interested in. Choose a subject and write a short article (say 200-300 words) about it. Write in a way that they will understand and enjoy.

Topic	Readers interested in it
Tone	Example
Language comments	Example

Editing

Mark in text	Mark in margin	Meaning
⊢	♂	delete (cut out)
⋏	⋏ + new letters or words	insert (put in)
⌒	⌒	join up
∼	∼	change round
⌐	⌐	start new line
≡	(cap)	change to capital
—	(l.c.)	change to small letter

When the editor receives the typewritten article from the author, she has to prepare it for printing. She corrects any mistakes and marks up the copy so that the typesetter will know how it should be printed. This process is known as copy-editing, and there are a set of standard marks that a copy-editor uses.

I first met Marty Manada of new in group yes but not now in tacky down town Scarbrough.

The group had just finished a very hot and sweaty gig at Joey's Palce and were reviving themselves with a few welcome Bacardi and cokes before moving on to another date. This time at the Switchblade and Cufflink Filey. (Not much of a rave-up there, I should think. Marty was lean mean and not particularly dangerous to know. More half-asleep, really. I asked him, 'What did you think of the gig ?' 'Not a lot.' And the band tonight ? 'Not a lot.' It was obvious that line of questioning wasn't going to get me very far.

I first met Marty Manada of new in-group 'Yes but not now' in tacky downtown Scarborough. The group had just finished a very hot and sweaty gig at Joey's Place and were reviving themselves with a few welcome Bacardi and cokes before moving on to another date. This time at the Switchblade and Cufflink, Filey. (Not much of a rave-up there, I should think.)

Marty was lean mean and not particularly dangerous to know. More half-asleep, really. What did he think of the gig ? 'Not a lot.' And the band tonight ? 'Not a lot.' It was obvious that line of questioning wasn't going to get me very far.

Nobody's seen Pacino in a long time not in a good movie. Hes one of thos stars who's magnitude has been sustained by the vcr revolution. Theres a hole couch-potato cult rounds Scarface and Salvadoran death squad partisans just love Pacino's Commie-killin coke king Tony monatana, if you believe Oliver Stone. 'Sea of Love', the big new romantic thrillerin which Pacina plays a homicide dteective who falsfor a murder
suspect (Ellen Barkin in an astinishingly steaming performance), is Paciono,s retrun to populra movie making; the public inception of his new post clandestine phase. In additon to 'Sea of lOve, hes done an uncharacteristically lioghthearted thing: an unrcedited cameo in Warren beatty's 'Dick tracy', due out this year, playingf a bad guy known as 'Big Boy' the Joker in the film.
'What is big about him,' explained Pacino one night in LA, where he was shooting 'Dock Tracey', 'is that he's the world's largest dwarf.'
He also sadi yes to Fances Coopolla after Coppola told him he'd come up wit a brand.now concept for a thirds Gidfather movei

Try your hand
You are the copy-editor. If you can get a photocopy of this part of the article, you can make your corrections on that. Otherwise you will have to begin by copying it out exactly as it is printed here.

1 Mark all the corrections using the signs on the opposite page.

2 Write out a version of the text as it will appear when all your corrections have been made.

Design

Every page in a magazine has to be planned. This involves thinking about questions like:

1 How many pictures ? and how big ?
2 How are the words going to fit on the page ?
3 What about colour ?
4 How can it all be made to look clear and attractive ?

Usually the designer starts by drawing sketches of the page **design**. Later on she has to work very accurately on the **layout** of the text and pictures.

TRIPLE BILL

Like three girls: Julia Roberts, Carre Otis and Jennifer Jason Leigh. With six movies out this year between them, Hollywood's hottest young actresses make the transition from starlet to star

JULIA ROBERTS

Julia Roberts has strong opinions on the way movie actresses should conduct themselves. 'If women didn't play the kind of women that they wouldn't hang out with, then there would be fewer of those roles,' she says. 'We wouldn't see so many surface cheesepuffs.'

She seems to be taking her own advice. In Mystic Pizza, a small-town girl buddy movie set among the Portuguese American community on the New England coast, she plays the smart, sassy waitress Daisy Araujo. And in the big budget female ensemble piece Steel Magnolias she is cast as Shelby, a wilful, wise-cracking southern belle.

Daisy wiggles her way through her job at the pizza parlour in the stifling, traditional community of Mystic, breaking off from dazzling the town's male population just long enough to swap gossip with her fellow waitresses, her younger sister Kat (played by Annabeth Gish, last seen in

Shag) and their childhood friend Jojo (Lili Taylor).

When she first heard about the film, Roberts assumed she was being tried out for the role of the lively but unglamorous Kat. Discovering her mistake, she panicked. 'I thought I looked wrong so I put some washable black dye in my hair and went and did the audition,' she says. 'My partner for the scene started to run his hands through my hair and all I could think of was how black his hands would be. After the audition, I walked out into the rain and the stuff ran down my face and down the back of my neck.'

Becoming a somewhat amateurish ravenhead didn't stand in her way – Roberts' spirited performance stands out in the gentle, low-key production.

Steel Magnolias is a different kind of film entirely. Anything but low-key, it's a melodramatic reworking of an off-Broadway play centring on the clients of a small-town Louisiana beauty parlour. It boasts several huge names: Dolly ▷

A spirited performance in Mystic Pizza brought Julia Roberts, far left, to the attention of Hollywood's major moguls, but for Jennifer Jason Leigh, above, with 15 feature films to her credit, public recognition has been a long time coming. Unwilling to play a victim, or become a victim of the dearth of good women's roles, Carre Otis, left, is going to write them herself

47

Your opinion

Look at the three magazine spreads on these two pages. For each one answer these questions:

1 What is the subject matter ?
2 What is the proportion of words and pictures ?
3 How have the pictures been used to strengthen the spread ?
4 Does it use different sized print, headings and boxes to make things clearer, bolder, livelier ?
5 How well does it use colour ?
6 How well does the whole design get across the message of the spread ?

When you have thought about each of the spreads, compare them and decide which you like best and why. (You could also work out which one came from each of the magazines on page 25 - and how you can tell.)

and layout

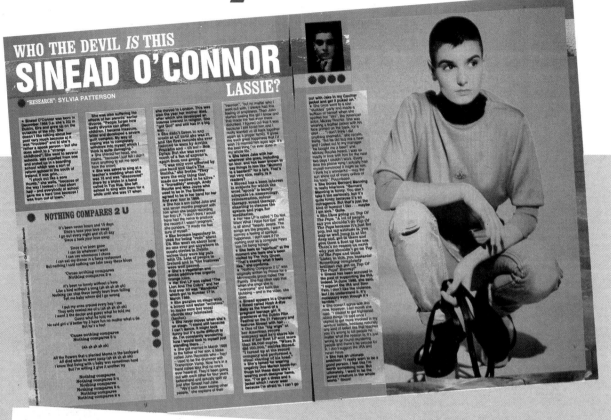

WHO THE DEVIL *IS* THIS
SINEAD O'CONNOR
LASSIE?

● "RESEARCH": SYLVIA PATTERSON

NOTHING COMPARES 2 U

It's been seven hours and 15 days
Since u took your love away
I go out every night and sit all day
Since u took your love away

Since u've been gone
I can do whatever I choose
I can see whomever I choose
I can eat my dinner in a fancy restaurant
But nothing I said nothing can take away these blues

'Cause nothing compares
Nothing compares 2 u

It's been so lonely without u here
Like a bird without a song
Nothing can stop these lonely tears from falling
Tell me baby where did I go wrong

I put my arms around every boy I see
They only remind me of u (ah ah ah oh)
I want 2 the doctor and guess what he told me
Guess what he told me
He said girl u'd better try to have fun no matter what u do
But he's a fool

'Cause nothing compare
Nothing compare 2 u

(Ah ah ah ah oh)

All the flowers that u planted Mama in the backyard
All died when he went away (ah ah ah oh)
I know that living with u baby was sometimes hard
I know that living with u baby I give it another try

Nothing compares
Nothing compares 2 u
Nothing compares
Nothing compares 2 u
Nothing compares
Nothing compares 2 u

JOOLS HOLLAND: SEASONED TRAVELLER

Jools Holland is no stranger to the rigours of travelling. Between touring Britain and America with Squeeze and the Jools Holland Big Band, and his various far-flung TV projects, Holland has learned that it's important to make the most of his time spent getting from A to B.

FEAR OF FLYING

The world keeps
shrinking and distant
lands get nearer and
nearer all the time.
This issue of BLITZ
celebrates the travel
urge — covering places
as far apart as Bali and
Berlin, Vietnam and
Disneyland. But it
starts here with
travel's most daunting
aspect — getting there.

REPORT PAUL MATHUR

PHOTOGRAPHS DAVID WOOLLEY

MAP STEVEN APPLEBY

JOOLS HOLLAND:
SEASONED TRAVELLER

Speaking and writing

Pronunciation and accent

People have strong attitudes towards spoken English. These include beliefs about the clarity with which people speak and the accents they use.

C I think it's very slaphappy : spoken English today.

D It has changed for the worse. It grates on us elder people the way our lovely English language has been disregarded. I mean I've got twenty-five grandchildren. It's a different way of teaching they've got today, haven't they ? We were taught the real old-fashioned way to pronounce our vowels and verbs and proverbs and all the rest of it. If we didn't do it we got chastised : we had to speak clearly or else we were told to sit down.

B If you don't speak clearly and pronounce your words properly then that's bad English. I think that's why you go to college to learn to speak - you know - the first class English, but if you go to an ordinary school...well anything could happen. You could learn English, but you won't pronounce it quite so thoroughly as what a student in a college would do.

E If you want to hear the finest English - spoken English - go to Invernessshire. The pronounciation (sic) of words is fantastic : it's clear. They'll tell you up there they speak the finest English and they do.

F I myself am aware that when I'm with strangers my accent tends to become more nearly British because I'm trying to be accepted and I'm trying to reduce the blocks to communication as much as I can. But if I get excited, or if I'm amongst friends, my American comes out and it's quite embarrassing to me. And in fact my children have pointed out that I tend to speak pidgin with foreigners and go all English with English people.

J I spent three weeks in America last summer and by the time I got back I was told that the way I spoke was actually quite different. The Americans were noticing that I had an American accent and the English noticed that my sentences went up at the end instead of down. Like if you say, 'Do you want a cup of tea ?' and it'd go down with the tea at the end. But if like when Catherine speaks or when the Americans speak it's like, 'D'you want a cup of tea ?'

K So, 'D'you want a cup of tea, eh ?' Yeah I do add 'Eh ?' to the end of sentences. That is a common trait of all New Zealanders. I didn't realise I was doing it until I came here.

1 These speakers use these words and phrases when discussing speech. What do you think each of them means ?

2 Apart from your own local accent, which regional accents do you find easy to understand ? Why do you think this is ?

3 Which accents do you find difficult to understand ?

4 What do you think are the most important things about the way we should speak to people ?

5 Is school the place to learn good speech ?

pronunciation

accent

the finest...spoken English

the real old-fashioned way to pronounce our vowels

pronounce it (English)...thoroughly

speak clearly

blocks to communication

wrong to write?

Some things are more easily communicated in speech than in writing...

...while other things are better written than spoken

Speech or writing ?

For each of the following purposes, say whether you think it would be better done in speech or writing and explain why.

1 Providing instructions to go with a new washing machine.

2 Explaining to a plumber the repair you want done in your kitchen.

3 Introducing two people to each other.

4 Making a will.

5 Announcing who is in the school football team.

6 Instructing a hairdresser how you want your hair done.

Either - both - neither

There are situations in which you can use either speech or writing...

Can you think of any other occasions when either speech or writing can be used ?

...occasions when people use both...

Can you think of any other occasions when both speech and writing are used ?

...and even times when we don't need to use either

Can you think of any other occasions when neither speech nor writing is necessary to communicate ?

34

Getting results

We can achieve different results by writing a letter, telephoning, or speaking to someone face to face.

CHAPTER 2

Maria and Jayne have just broken a window in nextdoor's house. They know they have to apologize. Should they:

- write a letter ?
- telephone ?
- go round and speak to their neighbour ?

1 Which would be easiest for them ?

2 Which would be most acceptable for the neighbour ?

3 Which would you do and why ?

Mrs Robinson has not had her dustbin emptied for three weeks. Should she:

- write a letter ?
- telephone ?
- go round to the Council Offices and try to speak to someone about it ?

1 Which would be easiest ?

2 Which would be most difficult or complicated ?

3 Which would be most likely to get results and why ?

Predicaments

Write ?
Telephone ?
Speak face to face ?
Which would you do, in these situations, and why ? (Remember you don't have to choose just one: you can always combine two, or even all three. If you do, you should explain how you would link them together.)

1 You have borrowed a much-loved record from a friend. On the way home from their house, you left it on the bus. Despite all your efforts you have been unable to get it back. You cannot afford to buy another to replace it. You have to tell your friend what has happened. What do you do ?

2 A local factory is looking for people aged 16-18 to do holiday work, putting soap into cardboard boxes in their packing department. The advertisement asks you to 'contact' Mrs Ryan, the Personnel Officer. You want to apply for the job. What do you do ?

Tom is describing a picture...

A

thereisabirdhangingupsidedowninwhatswhatloo
kslikeafactoryanditsbeenslaughterednitsitswings
arealltatterednhangingdownnitsheadsitsnecksbr
okenndumitsratherhorrificreallyandumthisisthes
ortofpicturethatmakespeoplethinkabouteatingthi
ssortoffoodlikechickensorwhatever

B

there is a bird hanging upside down in whats
what looks like a factory and its been
slaughtered n its its wings are all tattered n
hanging down n its heads its necks broken and
um its rather horrific really and um this is the
sort of picture that makes people think about
eating this sort of food like chickens or whatever

C

there is a...bird hanging upside down in
whats...what looks like a factory / and its been
slaughtered / n its its wings are all...tattered n
hanging down n its heads...its necks broken /
and um...its rather horrific really / andum...this
is the sort of picture that...makes people think
about eating...this sort of food like chickens or
whatever

D

There is a bird hanging upside down in what
looks like a factory. It's been slaughtered and its
wings are all tattered and hanging down. Its
neck's broken. It's rather horrific really; this is the
sort of picture that makes people think about
eating this sort of food (like chickens).

What is the difference ?

Look at the four versions of the description. They are all
saying much the same thing, but they do it in different
ways.

1 Read all four carefully.

2 What kind of differences can you see between A and B ?
Make a list of some of them.

3 What kind of differences can you see between B and C ?
Make a list of some of them.

4 What kind of differences can you see between C and D ?
Make a list of some of them.

What is the value ?

Each of the four is
based on what Tom
said. Listen to the
tape and then answer these questions:

1 Which of them is easiest to read
and understand ?

2 Why ?

3 Which of them gives the best
impression of what he said as
speech ?

SPEECH into writing

What Tom said about the picture shows us some of the ways in which speech differs from writing.

Hesitations

In ordinary conversation like this we make things up as we go along. Sometimes we need time to think, so we have to stop talking for a moment. We may just pause slightly:

> there is a...bird hanging upside down in whats...

Ums and ers

If we want to make it clear that we haven't finished - that we've got something more to say - then we may fill that pause with a noise that isn't a real word. These noises aren't meaningless. They are saying to the other person(s), 'Wait a moment. I've got something else to say and I'm just thinking it out.'

> its necks broken and um its rather horrific really and um

Word fillers

Sometimes the word 'and' does the same job - it fills in the spaces while we think what we are going to say next.

If Tom were writing a description of the picture, he would probably not write, 'and its been slaughtered and its wings are all tattered and hanging down and...' Similarly he would not repeat the word 'its' - this too fills in time while he thinks.

> and its been slaughtered n its its wings are all tattered n hanging down n

Making corrections

Speech happens very fast. Sometimes we make mistakes and have to correct ourselves.

Presumably Tom was going to say something like 'hanging upside down in what's obviously a factory...' He decides that is too strong, so instead he says, 'what looks like a factory...'

> hanging upside down in whats what looks like a factory

Changing course

Sometimes we start a sentence in one way and then decide that it would be better to put things differently, or even to talk about something else.

> its heads its necks broken

Exercise

1 How many of these points can you observe in this extract from the same conversation ?

2 Rewrite the extract following the pattern of sample D on the facing page.

yeah n i i agree with the killing of animals as long as all of its used n not really wasted because a lot is wasted when they slaughter animals so if the bits do go to a biology class to be cut up thats ok if its if the meat is being eaten then you may as well use the other parts for um scientific research

DIFFERENT GRAMMAR

Even when you get rid of all the features described on page 37, speech is very different from writing. Listen to the tape and read this extract:

```
well i just dont agree the way that theyre killed
they are kept and so i thought no i cant put up with
this any more so ill just eat veg eat vegetables cos
i mean id rather go out n um say with a gun kill a
pigeon myself  take it home pluck it skin it cook it
id rather do that than go to a supermarket and buy
this dead bird thats on display that you can just you
know like oh that ones not big enough i dont want
that one n ill have this one that hasnt got so much
fat on it or whatever
```

Even if we punctuate this and get rid of the features described on page 37, it still doesn't look completely like normal written English.

I just don't agree with the way that they're killed, they are kept and so I thought, ' No, I can't put up with this any more, so I'll just eat vegetables.' Because I'd rather go out with a gun, kill a pigeon myself, take it home, pluck it, skin it, cook it. I'd rather do that than go to a supermarket and buy this dead bird that's on display that you can just: 'Oh that one's not big enough I don't want that one. I'll have this one that hasn't got so much fat on it.'

Joining things up

Speech can join thoughts up in ways that don't work so well in writing. You can just put two thoughts 'side by side' and if you use the right tone of voice people will understand how you think they are linked. If we are going to join these ideas in writing, we have to add extra words.

The words we use to join sentences up are called conjunctions. They can join sentences for different purposes. Sometimes conjunctions join up to sentences like a plus sign:

Is there any difference between these two sentences ? If so, what ?

Conjunctions can also help us express more complicated ideas. They can help show:

I just don't agree with the way that they're killed, they are kept

I just don't agree with the way that they're killed ------ they are kept

and   or

I just don't agree with the way that they're killed and they are kept

I just don't agree with the way that they're killed or they are kept

when things happen - when, before, after
why things happen - because, since, as
where things happen - where, wherever

EXPLAINING

When we are speaking we can use words like 'because' in a general way to mean, 'What I am going to say next explains and fills out what I have just said.' When we use them in writing, we have to be more precise.

> i just dont agree the way that theyre killed they are kept and so i thought no i cant put up with this any more so ill just eat veg eat vegetables cos i mean id rather go out

I just didn't agree with the way that they're killed or the way that they are kept and so I thought, 'No I can't put up with this any more so I'll just eat vegetables.' The reason for this is that I'd rather go out...

REFERRING BACK

Sometimes it works the other way round. When we are making quite a detailed point, we may feel that we need to make things absolutely clear to the listeners. For example we may be afraid that they have forgotten the point of what we are saying. In this example Claire wants to make sure that we still know why she is giving this list of things she would be prepared to do. So she puts in the words,'I'd rather do that.' In writing we don't need to do that, because the reader can always just look back a few words to sort things out.

> id rather go out n um say with a gun kill a pigeon myself take it home pluck it skin it cook it id rather do that than go to a supermarket and buy

I'd rather go out with a gun, kill a pigeon myself, take it home, pluck it, skin it, and cook it than go to a supermarket and buy...

Looking at conjunctions

If you look at Tom's first piece of speech, you will see that these are the main things he says:

there is a bird hanging upside down in what looks like a factory
it has been slaughtered
its wings are all tattered and hanging down
its neck is broken
it is rather horrific really
this is the sort of picture that makes people think about eating this sort of food

These short sentences can be built up into longer sentences in a number of different ways:

There is a bird that has been slaughtered hanging upside down in what looks like a factory.
A bird has been slaughtered and it is hanging upside down in
what looks like a factory

How would you combine the remaining four sentences to make two longer sentences ?

How sentences work

TYPES OF SENTENCE

We can divide sentences into four groups according to how we use them:

Statement   I like ice cream.
Question   Do you like ice cream ?
Command   Buy me an ice cream!
Exclamation What a fantastic colour that ice cream is !

PARTS OF A SENTENCE

Simple sentences follow patterns. They are made of some or all of these basic parts.
Each part can consist of one word, or a group of words (a phrase).

Subject

He is my brother.
The people next door but three keep chickens.

The subject of the sentence usually comes at the beginning of statement sentences.

Verb

He **is** my brother.
She **will have been waiting** for ages.

The verb normally comes after the subject in a statement sentence.

Object

I dropped **it**.
She has been looking after **my uncle's cat**.

The object normally comes after the verb.

Adverbial

She threw it **away**.
We are going **to the pictures**.

The adverbial gives the answer to questions like:
    When ?
    Where ?
    How ?

Complement

They are **sisters**.
Charlotte is **captain of the basketball team**.

Like an object, a complement comes after the verb, but it is different in sentences like these examples, because the subject and the complement refer to the same person. You can see this by comparing these two sentences:
Mr Green met our postman. - SUBJECT+VERB+OBJECT
Mr Green is our postman. - SUBJECT+VERB+COMPLEMENT.

SENTENCE PATTERNS

Most English sentences follow a number of regular patterns. For example:

He	went	home.
My mother	is going	to the supermarket.
The person down the road	was walking	towards the traffic lights.

Verbs and time

The verb in a sentence gives us information about time:

past	present	future
I won a race yesterday.	*I am happy now.*	*I shall receive a prize tomorrow.*

Tense

The form of a verb that tells us about time is called the tense. These are examples of past tenses:

I ran well.
I was running for a long time.
I had run several races before this one.

Aspect

We also change the form of the verb to give other information. Compare these two sentences: They are both past tenses - what is the difference in the meaning we get from them ?

The aspect of the verb gives us information about how the speaker thinks or feels about the action being described. English tenses have three aspects:

These are examples of future tenses:

I shall visit her tomorrow.
I shall be going there by bus.

I ran for a long time.
I was running for a long time.

	Simple	Continuous	Perfect
Past	I ran	I was running	I had run
Present	I run	I am running	I have run
Future	I shall run	I shall be running	I shall have run

Sequence

In writing we normally keep the same verb tense when telling a story, for example:

Once upon a time there *was* a little girl called Red Riding Hood. She *lived* with her mother...

If we do not, it seems odd:

Once upon a time there *was* a little girl called Red Riding Hood. She *lives* with her mother...

In speech we may move from one tense to another without people being too concerned :

> i just *dont agree* the way that theyre killed they are kept and so i *thought*

The normal way of writing this would be:

> I just *didn't agree* with the way that they were killed or the way that they were kept and so I thought...

A written version

If you make all the changes described on page 37, the beginning of what Claire says becomes this:

> I just didn't agree with the way that they're killed or the way that they are kept and so I thought, 'No I can't put up with this any more so I'll just eat vegetables.' The reason for this is that I'd rather go out with a gun, kill a pigeon myself, take it home, pluck it, skin it, and cook it than go to a supermarket and buy this dead bird that's on display.

Unfortunately changing a piece of speech into a piece of writing is not as simple as that.

The right order

What we are left with is not a straight piece of writing. If you take what she says to pieces you can see that the points she makes don't follow on from each other in the way they should. There are four points·

> (a) I just didn't agree with the way that they're killed.
> (b) I just didn't agree with the way that they are kept.
> (c) I thought, 'No I can't put up with this any more so I'll just eat vegetables.'
> (d) I'd rather go out with a gun, kill a pigeon myself, take it home, pluck it, skin it, and cook it than go to a supermarket and buy this dead bird that's on display.

The way she says it sounds fine, but when it is written down we can see that these four points aren't in the right order. You can see this if you ask yourself, 'Which of them is a decision and which are reasons for that decision?' Then you can see that (a), (b) and (d) are the reasons for (c). The best order for them is b - a - d - c. So a more sensible way of writing the argument is:

> I just didn't agree with the way that animals are kept or killed. I felt that I would rather go out with a gun, kill a pigeon myself, take it home, pluck it, skin it, and cook it than go to a supermarket and buy this dead bird that's on display. As a result I thought, 'No I can't put up with this any more : I'll just eat vegetables.'

The awkward bits

The rest of what Claire says just doesn't work as writing whichever of these techniques we use:

When she says it we know what she means, because of the voice she puts on. She is imagining someone speaking at the supermarket

> That one's not big enough. I don't want that one. I'll have this one that hasn't got so much fat on it.

> that you can just you know like oh that ones not big enough i dont want that one n ill have this one that hasnt got so much fat on it or whatever

In writing this has to be explained:

> People treat them as things and say things like, 'That one's not big enough. I don't want that one. I'll have this one that hasn't got so much fat on it.'

Audience

The other important difference between speech and writing concerns the audience. When you are talking to someone you can keep an eye on the effect you are having on them. You can make sure that they are understanding what you are saying.

Making sure they understand

Listen to the tape and read the transcript carefully. Then think about the questions that follow.

1 What do you think Claire means when she says, 'They've got the lungs.' ?

2 What would she need to say to make this clear ?

3 Why do you think she doesn't do this ?

4 Who says, 'Ooh ooh ! How can you ? Ooh ooh !' ?

5 Who says, 'It's all disgusting.' ?

6 Are the answers to both (4) and (5) clear ? If not, how could she make them clearer ?

7 How would you write all this, so that it is clearer ?

you know people are saying theyll say you know like when we have biology and theyve got the lungs and they go ooh ooh how can you ooh ooh and its all disgusting

Getting the tone right

When you are speaking you can also notice very quickly if you are using the right tone.

Listen to the tape and read the transcript carefully. Then think about the questions that follow.

1 How would you describe Matthew's tone of voice ?

2 What does it tell us about his relationship with his audience ?

3 Would it be a suitable tone to use when speaking to a large audience of vegetarians ? What are the reasons for your answer ?

4 How would you write all this so that it is suitable to be read by people whom Matthew does not know and who may be vegetarians ?

Some people say that um that the lungs that youre using or whatever youre using to cut up is not is for scientific purposes and you dont actually need it but there again you need to eat meat some people say im not saying i agree with it but somell say that people need to eat meat and thats perfectly erm acceptable so what dyou say to that

The whole conversation

Tom

there is a bird hanging upside down in whats what looks like a factory and its been slaughtered n its its wings are all tattered n hanging down n its heads its necks broken and um its rather horrific really and um this is the sort of picture that makes people think about eating this sort of food like chickens or whatever

Matthew

well it brings um it just looks a bit horrible really just letting it die that way i dont think it should maybe itd be better if they just killed it straightaway

Tom	yeah broke its neck
Matthew	and not yeah and not
Tom	be a quick death
Matthew	yeah cos i dont its not very nice letting it you know perish letting it perish very slowly i couldnt think of anything worse hanging there

Claire

you know people are saying theyll say you know like when we have biology and theyve got the lungs and they go ooh ooh how can you ooh ooh and its all disgusting n this is what

Tom	and then theyll go home and eat and eat um a steak for tea or something
	(general talk)
John	explain what you mean
Tom	its like hypocritical to um to be disgusted by something like that and then go and eat something that's basically the same sort of thing
Matthew	some people
Claire	and they're not squirmish about it

Matthew	Some people say that um that the lungs that youre using or whatever youre using to cut up is not is for scientific purposes and you dont actually need it but there again you need to eat meat some people say im not saying i agree with it but somell say that people need to eat meat and thats perfectly erm acceptable so what dyou say to that
Tom	yeah n i i agree with the killing of animals as long as all of its used n not really wasted because a lot is wasted when they slaughter animals so if the bits do go to a biology class to be cut up thats ok if its if the meat is being eaten then you may as well use the other parts for um scientific research
Claire	id rather it all be like used up but i just dont like the way they are treated cos theyre kept in little boxes piled on top of one another and then theyre slaughtered in this horrible slow death and its just not fair cos its a life form n we you know like we evolved from the life forms
Matthew	it reminds me of battery hens you know because yeah i know but its let making them stay in however big the boxes are you know for all their life and just there to lay eggs it reminds me reminds me a bit of um the um hen that laid golden eggs in um in jack and the beanstalk because its kind its just kind of there just to lay eggs it hasnt got a life of its own
	(general talk)
John	lets change this a bit claire youre a vegetarian
Claire	well i just dont agree the way that theyre killed they are kept and so i thought no i cant put up with this any more so ill just eat veg eat vegetables cos i mean id rather go out n um say with a gun kill a pigeon myself take it home pluck it skin it cook it id rather do that than go to a supermarket and buy this dead bird thats on display that you can just you know like oh that ones not big enough i dont want that one n ill have this one that hasnt got so much fat on it or whatever
John	but you actually like meat
Claire	yes i love it i prefer it to see it alive n being well treated or free or something as opposed to being stuck in a little box
John	and and you youre a vegetarian but dyou eat eggs n milk
Claire	i eat free range eggs yes and milk i drink milk
John	and thats all right
Claire	yeah well i only think you can take these things so far n i th i wouldnt go fruitarian or something cos that seems a bit extreme

Writing it up

1 Choose a section of between five and ten lines that has not been used so far in this chapter. Follow the pattern of version D on page 36 and turn it into a piece of 'punctuated speech'. As you write it out get rid of the hesitations and other features mentioned on page 37.

2 Now write it again. This time pay attention to the points made on pages 38-41.

3 Finally make a third version. This time note the points on pages 42 and 43. Make a full written version for a chosen audience.

TALKING POINTS

What to do

The purpose of this piece of work is to follow the same pattern that Tom, Matthew and Claire did when they were talking about the factory farming picture on page 36. You should work in a group of two, three, or four. You will need to use a tape-recorder to record what is said. Make sure that you know how to use it - and that it is recording properly - before you begin.

1 Discuss

Turn on the recorder. Talk about the picture and your thoughts and feelings as you look at it.

2 Select

Choose one short section (of about 1-2 minutes) to work on.

3 Transcribe

Write down all the words everyone said. The easiest way to do this is to take one person each and write down that person's speech. Then you can join together to build up the group version.

4 Script

Choose one part of the discussion and work together to make a detailed written version of how the discussion went. Stay close to the words spoken, but follow the ideas on pages 36 and 37, so that you can develop a version that other people will be able to understand.

5 Opinion

Now work on developing part or all of your script into a full written argument. Remember the points that were made on pages 38-43. Write for other people in your English group and remember that they haven't been taking part in your discussion, so they don't know what was said.

summary

SPEAKING AND WRITING

People have strong opinions about what is right and wrong in other people's speech. These opinions often focus on clarity of pronunciation and accent. People often judge others by the way in which they speak as much as if not more than by the content of what they have to say.

WRONG TO WRITE ?

Although both speech and writing are used in a huge variety of situations, both have their strengths and weaknesses. Some situations call for spoken communication while there are others where writing is more effective. There are also a number of occasions when we communicate without either speech or writing.

TALKING PICTURES

There are many differences between speech and writing. A number of these arise from the fact that speech happens quickly: speakers frequently have to 'make it up as they go along.' So everyday speech often contains hesitations, 'ums and ers', filler words, corrections and changes of course.

DIFFERENT GRAMMAR

There are also broad grammatical differences between speech and writing. Speech does not need to make the links between ideas completely clear through grammar; we can often do this by tone of voice. When we write we make greater use of conjunctions like *because, when*, and *so* to link ideas and build sentences. On the other hand when speakers are discussing something complicated, they may need to explain things more fully than is necessary in writing. (The reader can always stop reading and look back - but this is impossible for the listener.)

HOW SENTENCES WORK

There are four types of sentence: statement, question, command and exclamation. Sentences follow patterns constructed of up to five components: subject, verb, object, adverb, complement. The verb in a sentence shows time through the tense, and aspect. Speech is not so strict about verb tense as writing is.

A WRITTEN VERSION

Speech is often shaped differently from writing, too. When we write we can take time to arrange ideas in the best order. In speech (especially in conversation and discussion) we may say things as they occur to us and link them to earlier ideas by the way in which we express them. We can also achieve all sorts of effects by our tone of voice which are impossible in writing. The writer has to spell such things out more fully.

project: *Community Service Volunteers*

This unit is about two girls, Kirsty and Melanie, who are working as Community Service Volunteers in Hereford and Worcester. They told us about their work and talked about its good points and its bad points. What they said is on the tape, and some of it is also printed on the next few pages. There are also photographs of them and the people they work with.

WHAT IS CSV ?

CSV is community service volunteers, so generally working for the community. You can work with people in borstals; you can work with in night shelters; you can do ILS, which is Independent Living Scheme - working with disabled people, or blind people, or deaf people. You can work with children in in sort of inner city areas; you can work in youth centres.

It's to introduce people - young people - I mean you can do CSV up to thirty five and there has been known people to do it over that age - but it's to sort of broaden people's minds. Because there is sort of things in this country that people aren't aware of.

CSV is for people to help people. You're not there for the money; you're there to help somebody know that you're being there. You're benefiting both for them and for you and, if you weren't there, their life wouldn't be worth...

You get very good experience. You learn a lot about yourself: how you can cope with different situations. And just being there it's worthwhile: you're cheering the other person up and you're getting a lot out of it by seeing them happy.

Activities

All the activities build up to a single piece of writing. At the end you will be asked to write an article for a teenage magazine about CSV and the work that Kirsty and Melanie are doing.

1 Listen to the tape and read the text.

2 Make a list of the main points the two speakers make about CSV. You may find it helps to use these headings.
- What volunteers do
- Who can do it
- What the point of it is
- What you get out of it

3 Use the notes you have made to write a short explanation of what CSV is.

1 Listen to the tape and look at the photographs.

2 Listen to the tape again. This time make notes on the most interesting and important things that Kirsty says. You may find it useful to use these headings.

3 Listen to the tape for a third time. As you listen, check through the notes you have made. Add any extra points you think are important.

sample headings

Glen
Glen's family
Work at the school
At Glen's home
Problems
Kirsty's working day
Kirsty's working week

WORKING AT ORCHARD STREET

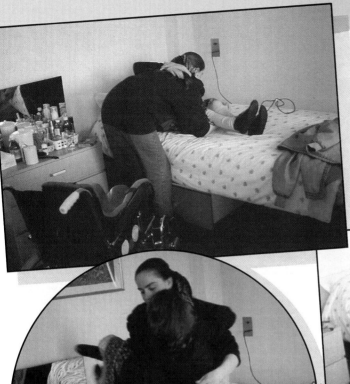

1 Listen to the tape and look at the photographs.

2 Listen to the tape again. This time make notes on the most interesting and important things that Melanie says. You may find it useful to use these headings.

3 Listen to the tape for a third time. As you listen, check through the notes you have made. Add any extra points you think are important.

sample headings

What staff do at Orchard Street
The demands it makes
The residents
Different types of disability
'Care' and 'facilitating'
Communicating

Note on spellings:
cerebral haemorrhage (stroke)   cerebral palsy (spastic)
paraplegic   tetraplegic   quadraplegic

Good days and bad days

good days are very good / the time goes quickly but it it depends really / Glen's so moody such a moody child...its...its difficult when hes being naughty and taking his clothes off and things like that / I do get fed up but its OK because I got a lot of support / I can talk to the supervisor / I can ring her up...discuss it with the family and then I go to school / theres lots of people to talk about it so its quite good...its not that bad

obviously its not all fun at orchard street / er because they are normal per- people they go have tempers just like everyone else / they have bad days like everyone else / they get crabby...and because theyve got like no one else to take it out on they take it out on the staff and the other residents / so some...but if they do start an argument with you you argue it through because you would do with everyone else / you don't think oh my god theyre disabled i shouldnt argue with them you you argue it out with them / you think well whats whats wrong with you what why why are you treating me like this / excuse me im not here to be treated like this / um...so you...so...but it upsets you obviously like any argument upsets you but youve got to argue it out otherwise you wont resolve anything / ...um and so you go can go home at the end of the day if its been a long day if youve done a lot of lifting if youve done a lot of physical work...um...because it is mentally demanding because...you have to concentrate all the time on what theyre saying...um...you are always there / you cant have even five minutes off really because youre forever on call...er...so you can go home at the end of the day and youre absolutely shattered /you really are tired and you just want to collapse / but some days youre just on such a high because youve had such a good day...um...ive had quite a lot of days like this / youve been out...ive been shopping with some

and weve had tea and weve been out for tea and cake or the residents take you out for lunch or youve gone to a pub for a drink with them and ... youve really had a good laugh and youve had um...although youve been working hard everybody's been in a good mood so... everybody's sat and watched neighbours and youve had a laugh and like we have a tea party on... every Tuesday we have a tea party so they take it in turns to buy a cake and we all sit and have a cup of tea and a piece of cake and and downstairs on level two they have a sunday roast which the staff from level three are usually invited down to and that was thats brilliant as well so some days we have a really good time / and you feel you just dont want to go home at the end of it you see / and you go home and youre on such a high that you think yeah you know / its a good laugh...brilliant

Working on the transcript

These pages contain all the words spoken by Melanie and Kirsty. They are transcribed without normal punctuation. (If you want to see the difference, compare them with the text on page 49, which has been sorted out and punctuated so that it is easier to read.)

1 Listen to the tape and read the text.

2 Now look at the text again and pick out some short sections that seem to you to sum up what the girls are saying.

3 Write them down, cut out all the hesitations and repetitions, and put in punctuation to make them clearer.

Writing the article

Now you are ready to write your article. You should have the following material:

1 An explanation of what CSV is.

2 Notes on how Kirsty helps Glen.

3 Notes on what Melanie does at Orchard Street.

4 Useful quotations summing up what the two of them think about their work.

As you write, remember your audience. Think about how much they know about this subject and what you can do to help them understand and to keep their interest.

Choosing illustrations

Your editor has told you that there is only space for three illustrations in this article: one large (the size of the photographs on page 50) and two small (the size of those on page 49). Which ones would you choose and why?

B If we go abroad on holiday you expect 'em to speak English. You havent got any trouble in making yourself clear. I mean you just go into a restaurant and they'll speak English as well as you.

Discussion points

1 Will they ?
2 Should they ?
3 How would the speaker feel if told that a Japanese had said, 'If we go abroad on holiday you expect 'em to speak Japanese' ?

A I think English is a world language and absorbs words from every other country, so you've got a vocabulary in English - it's got millions of words in it.

B I've often thought to myself, 'Well now, England has been invaded by various countries: the Romans and and French and so forth. Now I can't understand why we don't talk Italian. How did the English language get formulated ?' That's puzzled me: England, little tiny country, 'gainst all the world and everybody wants to learn English !

G

'Hospitalization' for instance - the American way of speaking. I think thats all wrong. Well - 'hospitalization' - there's never such a word, was there ? Am I right or am I wrong ? And all those '-izations' : Americans are always doing that, aren't they ?

-ization

The introduction of new words from other languages - especially from American English - can make people very cross. This speaker, like many people, objects to the American style of coining new words by adding the suffix -**ization**:

hospital --> hospitalize --> hospitalization

1 What do **hospitalize** and **hospitalization** mean ?

2 Do you object to them ?

3 What other -**ization** words have you come across ?

4 New words are constantly being invented. What examples of new, or 'in' or fashionable words can you think of ?

5 Do you think it is possible to make rules about which new words are acceptable and which ones are not ?

What this chapter is about

All languages change and develop through history; no language can just stand still. English has a very rich history - as we can see when we study its vocabulary.

You can find out the history of words by looking in a dictionary. Most medium- and large-sized dictionaries contain information about the **derivation** of words: where they come from.
Of course the story of English is not just the history of where the words came from; it is also about how the grammar, and spelling, and even pronunciation changed. Of these different elements the words are the most obvious and in many ways the most interesting.

All, and, through :
Old English words from the language of the people who invaded Britain in the 5th century.

languages, change :
French word from the language of the Normans who invaded Britain in the 11th century.

develop:
word that came from French in the 17th century

history :
word that came from Latin in the 15th century

Test out this theory about English.

1 Take a dictionary and see how many words you can find in five minutes that have been 'absorbed from other countries'.

2 Take four dictionary pages and work out what percentage of the words have been 'absorbed from other countries'.

A story of invasions

English was introduced into the British Isles by a group of tribes from North-East Europe, the Angles, the Saxons and the Jutes who invaded Britain in the 5th Century. They were farmers and settled in much of what we now call England.

Many of the original inhabitants of this area lost their lands, and their language, Celtic was rejected by the settlers. As a result it was pushed into Scotland, Wales and Cornwall, where it survived and developed into Scots Gaelic, Welsh and Cornish.

Some words from Old English

① Hæfst þu hafoc ?

"Have you a hawk ?"

② Ic hæbbe

"I have."

③ Canst þu temian hig ?

"Do you know how to tame them ?"

④ Gea, ic cann. Hwæt sceoldon hig me buton ic cuþe temian hig ?

"Yes, I do. What use would they be to me if I could not tame them ?"

The English spoken by the Anglo-Saxon settlers was very different from the language we speak today, as you can see from this short conversation in Old English. It comes from an Old English textbook called *Aelfric's Colloquy*. How many of the words are similar to modern English ones ?

Translating

If you compare the Old English and Modern English versions, you should be able to work out what some of the Old English words mean. Copy out this table and fill in the spaces.

Old English	Modern English
Hæfst þu ?	
hafoc	
	I have
Canst þu ?	
	Yes
	I know how to
Hwæt	

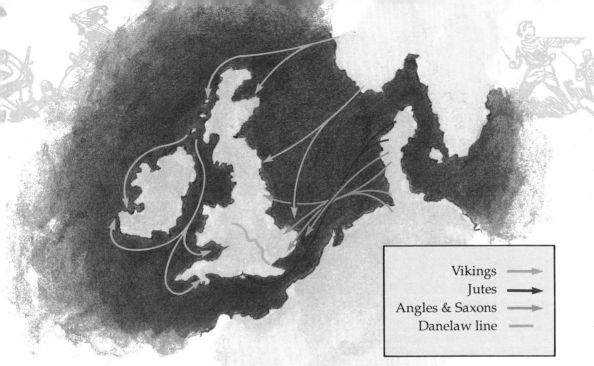

Vikings	⟶
Jutes	⟶
Angles & Saxons	⟶
Danelaw line	—

THE VIKINGS

During the 8th century new invaders, the Vikings, began to attack England. They came from Scandinavia and attacked the east coast of England. By about 950 they controlled half the country. They would probably have gone much further, if it had not been for the young leader of the English kingdom of Wessex: King Alfred. Alfred and the men of Wessex defeated the Danes, as they called them, at the Battle of Ethandune in 878. By the Treaty of Wedmore Alfred and the Danes agreed to divide England between them. The border they chose was an old Roman Road, Watling Street, that ran from London to Chester. The Danes would control the area to the north and east, while the south and the west were left to the English.

The Danes spoke their own language. It was not completely different from Old English, so speakers of the two languages could just about understand each other. Even so, they were different languages with different words and grammar. As a result many words came into Old English from Old Norse, the language of the Danes. Many of them are very common words:

call	fellow	get	hit
husband	law	leg	low
root	same	take	want
wrong	skin (and many other words that begin sk-)		

Research

Use a dictionary to find other words that come from Old Norse. Make a list of them.

Doubling up

With words being borrowed from another language, it was not long before English began to have two words for the same thing:

Old English	Old Norse
rear (a child)	raise (a child)
wish	want
craft	skill
hide	skin

What is the difference ?

Think about the differences between the words in each pair. Sometimes it shows more clearly in words derived from them.

1 What is the difference between calling someone 'crafty' and calling them 'skilful' ?

2 When would you use the word 'hide' to describe the skin of an animal ?

3 Think about the different ways in which we use the words 'wish' and 'want'. Make up a group of sentences that illustrate the differences between them.

Norman French

The next major influence on English began in 1066, when Duke William of Normandy led a small army of French-speaking knights across the Channel and defeated King Harold at the Battle of Hastings. The Normans were an army of occupation and soon controlled the government, the land and the church. As a result of this invasion there were three languages in use in England:

French spoken by the king and his court
Latin spoken by the leaders of the church
English spoken by the ordinary people

But the Norman rulers of England were few in number and of course they had to communicate with ordinary people. So gradually English became stronger until by the middle of the 14th century it was in use more or less everywhere.

Between 1066 and 1350 French was an important language and during that time many French words came into English, for example:

advise	command	govern
parliament	people	reign
sovereign	castle	

DOUBLING UP

As had happened before, the influence of French meant that there are often two words in English with similar meanings, one from Old English and one from Norman French:

Choose one of the pairs. Make up two sentences, each containing one of the words, showing how it is used. Compare the two sentences and explain what you think is the difference between the two - if any.

Old English	Normal French
kingly	royal
rise	ascend
keep	retain
ask	question
time	age
wish	desire

Middle English

As a result of such changes, English had changed. Old English had become Middle English. This is the name given to the form of English used between about 1150 and 1500. As you saw on page 58, Old English is like a foreign language. Middle English looks much more like the English we speak today.

GEOFFREY CHAUCER

One of the reasons why we know so much about Middle English is that we have a lot of literature, especially poetry, written in it. The most famous English poet of the period was Geoffrey Chaucer, who wrote the collection of stories in prose and verse called *The Canterbury Tales*. The stories were told by a group of pilgrims on their way to the shrine of St Thomas at Canterbury. At the beginning Chaucer describes each of the pilgrims. Among them was a wealthy townswoman, the Wife of Bath:

Hir hosen weren of fyn scarlet reed,
Her stockings were a fine scarlet red

Ful streite yteyd, and shoes ful moiste and newe.
Stretched tightly over the leg, and shoes moist and new

Boold was hir face, and fair, and reed of hewe.
Her face was bold and fair and red in colour

She was a worthy womman al hir live:
She had been a worthy woman all her life

Housbondes at Chirche dore she hadde five,
She had married five husbands in Church

Withouten oother compaignye in youthe, -
Not to speak of the company she kept when she was younger

But therof nedeth nat to speke as nowthe.
But we don't need to go into that just now

CHAPTER 3

Now you try

This is the beginning of the tale told by the Reeve. (A reeve was a person who managed a landowner's estates.) See if you can work out what it means.

At Trumpingtoun, nat fer fro Cantebrigge,
Ther gooth a brook, and over that a brigge,
Upon the whiche brook ther stant a melle;
And this is verray sooth that I yow telle:
A millere was ther dwellinge many a day.
As any pecok he was proud and gay.

Making one language

In about 1476 William Caxton set up the first printing press in England - in the precinct of Westminster Abbey. He was himself a writer and he translated books from Latin and French, as well as publishing the work of poets like Chaucer. When Caxton began work he realised that he was faced with a problem: there was not one English language, but many. He himself came from Kent where, he said 'is spoken as broad and rude (rough) English as is in any place of England.' People from other parts of England spoke dialects so different that they actually didn't understand each other. Caxton tells a story about some merchants who were waiting to travel to Holland. There was no wind, so they went ashore to look for food. They were not in their own area, so they could not make themselves understood:

What is it about ?

1 Read the story and work out what it means. Retell it in modern Standard English.

2 The word mercer means someone who buys and sells cloth. Are there any other words in Caxton's story that are difficult or unusual ? Why is the passage more difficult to read than modern English ?

one of theym named Sheffelde, a mercer, cam in-to an hows and axed for mete; and specyally he axyd after eggys. And the goode wyf answerde, that she coude speke no frenshe. And the marchaunt was angry, for he also coude speke no frenshe, but wolde have eggys, and she understode him not. And then at laste a nother sayd that he wolde have eyren. Then the good wyf sayd that she understod hym wel.

mete : food

A STANDARD LANGUAGE

Not only was English very varied, it was also still developing rapidly. Not many people could read, so it was mainly a spoken language. As a result, people spelled words differently - often in the same piece of writing. Caxton made decisions which had an important effect on the development of the language:

1 He chose one version of English - that of London and the South-East - as his standard. This meant that this became the language of printed English.

2 He tried to standardize the spelling of words. In the books he printed, most words are spelled in the same way all the time. (This meant that spelling stopped changing so fast and gradually became fixed.)

1 Why was it important to choose one dialect of English for printed books ?

2 Why do you think he chose the dialect of London and the South-East ?

3 Why is it necessary to have a standard spelling ? What would happen if spelling were not standardized ?

A national language

Many things contributed to the development of a national language in England. Two very important events were the translation of the Bible and the publication of the Book of Common Prayer. During the 17th century almost everyone went to church and so everyone heard each week the words of these two influential books. If we read the translation of the Bible published at the beginning of the 17th century, we can get an idea of what English was like at that time. If we compare it with a modern translation, we can see how much the language has changed.

1611

And the Jews' Passover was at hand, and Jesus went up to Jerusalem.
And found in the temple those that sold oxen and sheep and doves, and the changers of money sitting:
And when he had made a scourge of small cords, he drove them all out of the temple, and the sheep, and the oxen; and poured out the changers' money and overthrew the tables;
And said unto them that sold doves, Take these things hence; make not my father's house an house of merchandise.

King James Bible

1985

And the Jewish Passover was coming, so Jesus went up to Jerusalem. And he found people selling cattle and sheep and pigeons in the sanctuary, and the moneychangers sitting at business; so he made a whip out of cords and threw them all out of the sanctuary, sheep and cattle and all, and he flung down the money of the moneychangers and overturned their tables; and he said to the pigeon-sellers, Take these out of here, do not make my father's house into a house of business.

The Holy Gospel of John translated by Peter Levi

CHAPTER 3

Comparisons

Make a comparison between these two versions of the same story:

1 Some of the words have changed. For example **dove** becomes **pigeon**. Make a list of other changes of vocabulary.

2 Expressions have changed, too: **was at hand** becomes **was coming**. Find other examples.

3 The 1611 version also puts words in a different order at times: for example the position of the words in the temple in the second sentence. Try to find other examples of this.

Other things have changed, too

With this ring I thee wed, with my body I thee worship, and with all my worldly goods I thee endow

I give you this ring as a sign of our marriage. With my body I honour you, all that I am I give to you, all that I have I share with you

LATIN

Latin has influenced English in very important ways. This influence began at the time of the Roman Empire and is still continuing today.

A small number of English words date right back to the Roman Empire. They were taken up by the Germanic tribes whom the Romans conquered. These tribes included the Angles and Saxons who later invaded Britain.

mile   street   pound   sack

At the end of the 6th century AD, missionaries came from Rome and converted the English to Christianity. Latin was the language of their church and so many words began to come into English from Latin

cook   font   pope   school   angel

English

chance   legal   judge   royal

agile   habitual   capsule   gravity

When the Normans invaded England in 1066, they brought with them a language, Norman French, that had developed from Latin. As English changed under the influence of Norman French, it absorbed many more words from Latin.

During the 16th and 17th centuries, there was a rapid growth in science and the arts, known as the Renaissance. People studied the language and literature of ancient Greece and Rome. When they wanted to create new words they borrowed from Greek and Latin.

derivations : research

You will need a dictionary big enough to show you word derivations

1 Go through four pages looking at the derivation of each word.

2 Count the number that come from Latin, either directly, or through other languages.

3 Count the total number of words.

4 Work out the percentage of Latin words on the pages you have been using.

ALTERNATIVES

Because of the way in which English has taken words from Latin, we often have a choice of words, between 'Latin' words and 'Anglo-Saxon' words:

Latin	Anglo-Saxon
people	folk
ancestor	forebear

Explorations

The 16th and 17th centuries were a time when Europe 'expanded'. Explorers, sailors, soldiers, and missionaries travelled from England, France, Holland, and Spain east and west in search of new countries to explore and conquer. They took with them their religion, their weapons - and their language.

Shakespeare based much of the detail of his play *The Tempest* on accounts of expeditions to the Caribbean. One of the characters is Caliban, 'a salvage (savage) and deformed slave'. In this scene he speaks to Prospero his master, who has come to the island where Caliban lives and taken it over. The other character is Miranda, Prospero's daughter.

This island's mine, which thou tak'st from me. When thou cam'st first, thou strok'st me, and made much of me. And then I lov'd thee, and show'd thee all the qualities o' th'isle.

Curs'd be I that did so for I am all the subjects that you have, which first was mine own King: and here you sty (imprison) me in this hard rock, whiles you do keep from me the rest o' th' island.

Thou most lying slave, whom stripes (blows) may move, not kindness ! I have us'd thee, filth as thou art, with human care; and lodg'd thee in mine own cell, till thou did'st seek to violate the honour of (rape) my child.

I pitied thee, took pains to make thee speak, taught thee each hour one thing or other.

You taught me language; and my profit on't is, I know how to curse. The red plague rid you for learning me your language !

1 What does this scene tell us about what the early colonists thought of the inhabitants of the lands they visited ?

2 How does Caliban describe Prospero's approach to the local inhabitants ?

3 What does the scene tell us about the Europeans' attitudes towards
(a) local languages
(b) English ?

4 What are Caliban's thoughts about English ?

BEG, BORROW OR STEAL

English has taken words from all over the world. Words taken from other languages are known as 'borrowings' or 'loan words' - but we never give them back !

anorak
bonanza
cowboy
igloo
wigwam

bungalow
curry
juggernaut

smuggler
yacht

cafe
colonel
detail
entertain
envelope

broccoli
lottery
macaroni
piano
solo

boomerang
budgerigar
outback

Where do these come from ?

All these words have been borrowed from the areas marked on the map. Which words come from where, and what makes you think so ?

balcony	lassoo	stampede
battery	meringue	thug
brochure	moustache	totem
carnival	passport	tube
cruise	pioneer	vase
fanfare	pizza	vehicle
hustle	portrait	verandah
jungle	ranch	version
kayak	restaurant	walkabout
knapsack	spaghetti	wallaby

Research

Using a dictionary and keeping your eyes open as you move around, make a list of words that have come into English from other languages. You will probably find these areas of life good places to look:

    food (and eating out)
    clothes and fashion
    music

D.I.Y Word kit

Another way that words come into a language is that they are invented; for example, when a new scientific discovery is made. This process of inventing words is sometimes called coining.

When new words are invented, they tend to follow patterns. If we understand how some of these patterns work, we can often make a good guess about what new words mean - and how they are spelled.

BEGINNINGS

English is rich in prefixes. These are groups of letters which can be added to an existing word or stem to change its meaning or its use and so make a new word: dis + agree --> disagree

anti-	infra-	non-	re-
auto-	inter-	over-	sub-
bi-	micro-	poly-	super-
co-	mini-	post-	trans-
dis-	mis-	pre-	ultra-
ex-	mono-	pro-	un-
hyper-	multi-	pseudo-	under-
			uni-

ALL GREEK TO ME

There is another group of word components that come from Greek and Latin and are used a lot in constructing words. Some only come at the beginning or end of a word, but many can come in different places:

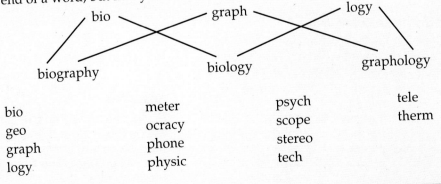

bio	meter	psych	tele
geo	ocracy	scope	therm
graph	phone	stereo	
logy	physic	tech	

COMPOUNDING

Another way of constructing new words is to join up two existing words to make a new one. This is called compounding:

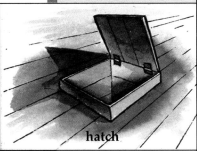
hatch

hatchback

back

age-old

birdbrain

birdcage

blackbird

cartwheel

extend

fathead

flowerbed

flypaper

foolproof

good-looking

home-made

homesick

lip-read

loudmouth

oven-ready

paperback

pinbrain

rock-hard

scarecrow

sea-green

sleep-walk

spring-clean

typewriter

What do they mean ?

Look at the list of 'Beginnings'. Choose five to work on. For each one:
1 Find at least two words that contain this beginning.
2 Explain what each word means.
3 Think about how the prefix is used, and explain what you think it means.

Some inventions

Some of these words exist and some of them have been invented. What do you think each of them might mean ?

biocracy	graphophone	stereograph
biometer	phonology	thermograph
geophone	psychograph	thermoscope

Invent a word

Now it is your turn. Use any of the methods described on this page to make up words for any of the following:

1 A machine for measuring how happy people are.

2 A vehicle that travels very slowly.

3 A new fuel made from recycled trainers.

4 A dog that is a cross between a poodle and an Alsatian.

Taking WORDS to pieces

Word families

Organize these words into three groups and explain why you have arranged them in the way you have:

managerial   frightenable   frightful
frighteningly   manageable   manager
impersonate   personalize   frightfully
personal   frighten   managed
fright   management   personality
managing   frightener   manageably
personable   manageress   impersonation
personify   personalization

Anatomy of a word

The fact that you were able to divide the words into three groups was because you recognized that English words come in **families**. The family of **person** can be presented like this:

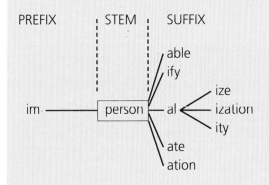

Now you try

1 Draw similar diagrams for the other words in the list at the top of the page.
2 Make up similar diagrams for as many of these stems as you can:
   doubt
   fear
   hate
   lone
   note
   order
   show
   teach
   write
   (You may have to make one or two minor changes in spelling.)

Meanings

1 Using a dictionary when necessary, make sure that you know the meaning of all the words in the **manage** family.
2 Take four other words in the family and explain how the meanings of each are linked to the meaning of the stem **manage**.

3 For each of the words you chose, try to work out how the prefix and/or suffix(es) have worked to build on the meaning of the stem.
4 Now do a similar thing with one of the other families you have worked on.

 # Suffixes

Suffixes have two main uses:

1 to change the word so that it fits the grammar of the sentence;

2 to change a word from one class to another. (Word classes are explained in full on page 85.)

Grammar

How should the words in brackets be changed so that the sentences are grammatically correct ?

a *There are 29 (child) in our class at school and about two thirds of our (teacher) are (woman).*

b *As we were (go) across the park we (chase) the (duck).*

c *Peter (write) better (story) than I do.*

Now think about the answers you worked out.

1 What word classes do the words in brackets belong to ?

2 What letter(s) did you add to the words in each class and why ?

CHANGING WORDS

These are examples of how we can use suffixes to change a word from one class to another.

inhabit -> inhabitant
break -> breakage
write -> writer
refuse -> refusal
arrange -> arrangement
happy -> happiness
beauty -> beautiful

fool -> foolish
wealth -> wealthy
drink -> drinkable
smooth -> smoothly
home -> homewards
deaf -> deafen
simple -> simplify
modern -> modernize

 CROSS REFERENCE

If you want more information about word classes, look on page 85. There are short explanations on pages 93 and 94.

Work it out

Explain what is going on in these changes, by copying and completing this table:

Original word	Word class	New word	Word class 2	Suffix	What it does
inhabit	*Verb*	inhabitant	*noun*	*-ant*	*verb → noun*
break		breakage			
write		writer			
refuse		refusal			
arrange		arrangement			
happy		happiness			
beauty		beautiful			
fool		foolish			
wealth		wealthy			
drink		drinkable			
smooth		smoothly			
home		homewards			
deaf		deafen			
simple		simplify			
modern		modernize			

English
A WORLD LANGUAGE

English is now the mother tongue of more people throughout the world than any other language except Chinese. Over 300,000,000 speak it as a first language (the language that they learn from their mothers). Probably a billion or more people speak it as a second language. (A second language is used by people in countries where there are several first languages as a means of communicating with each other.)

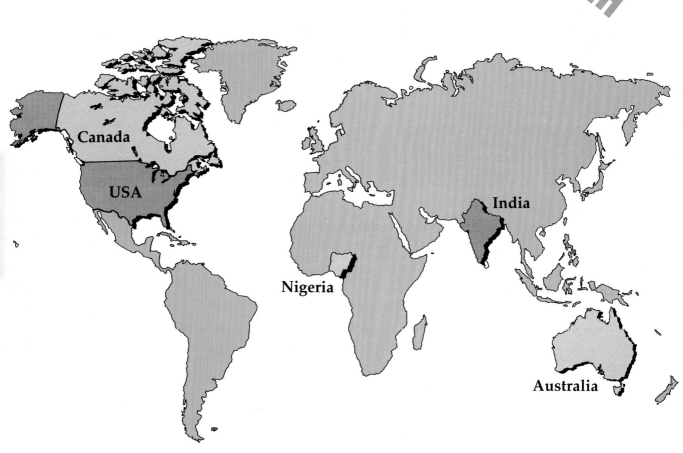

The map on this page shows some of the larger countries where English is spoken as a first or second language. The panels on page 73 tell you how English came to that country and also give information about how it is used there. Which panels belong to which country?

Out of a population of over 230 million, the vast majority speak English as their first language.

The settlement of this country began around 1600, although European sailors first reached it some time before that. Although settlers came from many European countries, and Spanish and French were widely used, English prevailed and became the national language.

Colonized by the British and the French. After a lengthy conflict, the British were successful and so English is the major national language. French is, however, the first language in certain areas.

A British colony until 1960. So English was used as the language of government. The main first languages are Ibo, Yoruba and Hausa.

Around 17 million of the total population of about 24 million speak English as their mother tongue. Most of the rest speak French as their first language.

Captain James Cook first landed here in 1770. The country was colonized by the British, who used it in the early years as a penal colony - a place to send convicts as a punishment.

English first came to this country in the early 17th century, when merchants set up trading centres in Madras and Calcutta. Eventually it became a British colony, with English as the language of government, and gained its independence in 1948.

It is not known how many people in this large West African country speak English as their first language. It is very widely used as a second language, and has official status as a national language.

This huge and highly populated country (over 700 million) has a bewildering number of languages. English is used as an official national language, alongside Hindi.

Nearly all the population of about 15 million speak English as their first language. The exceptions are mainly aboriginals in the Northern Territories and recent immigrants, especially from South-East Asia.

summary

A STORY OF INVASIONS

English is originally a Germanic language. Tribes from North-Western Europe invaded Britain in the 5th century AD. The language they spoke, Old English, is the basis of modern English. From the 8th century, new invasions took place. The Vikings, who settled parts of Eastern England spoke a Scandinavian language which influenced the development of Old English.

NORMAN FRENCH / MIDDLE ENGLISH

The Normans, who conquered England in 1066, spoke French, which became the language of government. English remained the language of the mass of ordinary people. Gradually French was used less and less, but although English became the national language it had been heavily influenced by French. The English spoken between the Norman Conquest and the middle of the 15th century is known as Middle English.

MAKING ONE LANGUAGE / A NATIONAL LANGUAGE

During the 15th century there were many different and conflicting dialects of English. With the influence of printing, the development of one national dialect - later to be known as Standard English - began. This process was continued by the publication of influential books such as the Authorized Version of the Bible and The Book of Common Prayer during the 16th and 17th centuries.

LATIN

Latin has influenced English over many centuries. There were Latin words in the language of the Anglo-Saxon invaders of Britain. After the conversion of much of Britain to Christianity in the 6th and 7th centuries, more Latin words entered Old English. Norman French had developed from Latin, so many of the words which entered English after the Conquest had originally come from Latin. Latin remained a source for new words during the period of the Renaissance.

EXPLORATIONS

With the expansion of Europe, which began in the 15th century, but accelerated in the 16th and 17th centuries, English was exported to America and to Asia and Africa.

BEG BORROW OR STEAL

As English speakers travelled to countries all over the world they acquired new words and expressions which then became part of the language. This process is still going on : new loan words continue to enter the language.

D-I-Y WORD KIT

Prefixes can combine with the stem of a word to make words with a new meaning. A number of very useful prefixes have come into English from Greek and Latin. New words are also coined by making compounds of two or more existing words.

TAKING WORDS TO PIECES

All words contain a stem. Words may also contain prefixes, which come before the stem, and suffixes which come after the stem. Words with the same stem can be grouped together in families. Suffixes work to change the form of a word so that it fits in with the grammar of the sentence. They can also change a word from one class to another.

ENGLISH - A WORLD LANGUAGE

The process of colonization and expansion continued until the beginning of the 20th century. As a result English is the dominant World language, spoken as a first language by a third of a billion people and as a second language by three or four times that number.

project: *Words in action*

You can get a very clear picture of the way in which language has changed over the centuries if you examine the ways in which playwrights have used words in the action of their plays. This project looks at the beginnings of four plays, covering a period of five hundred years.

1974

SCENE ONE. Interior. Prison cell: dawn

The cell is dark, except for the square of light from a small window. A MAN'S head moves into position in front of the window. His name is MAREK. We see him from the back.

SCENE TWO. Exterior. Prison yard: dawn.

We see MAREK'S face looking down into the yard. Against a wall at right-angles to his block, a PRISONER stands waiting to be executed. A FIRING SQUAD is at the ready. An OFFICER gives the order to fire, and the PRISONER slumps dead. Close-up MAREK'S face at the window.

SCENE THREE. Interior. First-floor London sitting-room: morning.

The room of a writer. Books, desk, typewriter, anglepoise lamp, a wall-board with various photographs, cards and pieces of paper pinned on it. One large easy leather chair. By one wall a long comfortable couch in dark corduroy. Also a long trestle table with wire trays, a small desk, filing cabinet, rows of manuscript neatly laid down.
A WOMAN stands at the high window, looking into the street. She is smoking and looking down. Her name is OLIVIA.

SCENE FOUR. Exterior. London street: morning.

Close-up Olivia at her window. In the street, MAREK stands searching wildly in his pockets. As he does so, he turns slowly on his feet. He pulls from his pockets bits of paper and thrusts them back. Obviously he can't find what he is looking for. He suddenly goes still, looking vacantly in front of him.

SCENE FIVE. Interior. First-floor London sitting-room: morning.

OLIVIA sits at her desk, stubs out her cigarette and picks up the microphone of a tape-recorder.
OLIVIA: Certainly Marek hasn't changed much. There he stands in the street, confused . . . absent-minded . . . short-sighted . . . going through his pockets. (Pause.) I wonder what he's lost this time? His passport? The address he was heading for? Matches? Cigarettes? (Pause.) Perhaps nothing at all, really. I've seen him do that before when he was gaining time after some dread or fear or memory had crossed his mind.

ACTIVITIES

1 This extract tells us some of the background to the story, especially about Marek, the central character. How much can you work out from these scenes ?

2 Look at the language used in scenes 1-4. How does it differ from ordinary storytelling ? Why do you think this is ?

3 Look at the language used by Olivia. Much of it is not in full sentences. What is the effect of this ?

4 Why does the writer make Olivia speak in this way ?

1863

In the 19th century, the theatre was a very popular form of Entertainment in London and other cities. The *Ticket-of-leave man* is based on a French story and is about how a man discharged from prison is not allowed to forget his crime.

SCENE. The Bellevue Tea Gardens, in the south-west suburbs of London. Summer evening. Front of the tavern with ornamental verandah, up L.; arbours along the stage, R. and L., with tables and seats; trees, shrubs, statues, &c. at the back, with ornamental orchestra and concert room.

PARTIES, male and female, seated at the different tables, R. and L.; WAITERS serving refreshments. Music heard off. As the curtain rises the parties are heard giving their orders; MALTBY moving about with an eye to the GUESTS, WAITERS &c.; two DETECTIVES at table, up L.C.

1st PARTY: Three hots with -----

WAITER [*serving another table*]: Yes, sir. Brandy and soda for you, sir.

2nd PARTY: Tea for four - shrimps and a muffin.

WAITER: Coming! [*Serving another party*.] Pot of half-and-half for you, sir. [At DETECTIVES' table.] Two Sherry negus two shillings. [*Takes money*]

MALTBY [*moving about*]: Now, James, three teas and a muffin in 5. - Jackson, money in 6. [*To a guest*.] Uncommon thirsty weather, sir, uncommon. [*To another party*.] If I might recommend a cobbler for the lady, sir, delicious refreshment for July. Now, James, look after them brandies in 3. [*Moves off, L.U.E.*]

[*Enter HAWKSHAW, R.1 E., he strolls carelessly to the* DETECTIVES' *table, then in an undertone and without looking at them*.]

HAWKSHAW: Report.

1st DETECTIVE [*in same tone and without looking at* HAWKSHAW]: All right.

HAWKSHAW [*same tone*]: Here's old Moss. Keep an eye on him. [*Strolls off, L.*]

[*Enter MOSS, R., sits at table*, R. 1 E.]

MOSS [*to the* WAITER]: Good evening, James. Four penn'orth of brandy, if you please, James. [*Sits, chair R.*] and a little peppermint. [*Coughs, and looks around*.] Tiger not here yet.

[*Bell rings*]

MALTBY: The concert bell, ladies and gentlemen - in the Rotunda. [*Pointing to the concert room*.] The first talent - selections from the best classical music. This way.

[Exit MALTBY, towards concert room R.]

negus : a drink made of wine, sugar, lemon, spice and hot water
cobbler : a drink made of wine, sugar, lemon and crushed ice

Activities

1 What impression do you get of the scene from reading this extract ?

2 In what ways does the language of this scene differ from modern English ?
 - quote the words that are different
 - explain what the modern English would be.

3 Some people might say that this scene is quite 'modern'; others might find it 'old-fashioned'. What do you think ?

1606

In the time of Shakespeare (1564-1616), there were permanent theatres used by companies of professional actors. Playwrights wrote about a very wide range of subjects: comedies, tragedies, and histories based on true life stories, ancient Greek and Roman literature, as well as stories from France, Italy and other parts of Europe. This extract comes from the beginning of one of Shakespeare's best known plays, *Macbeth*. It takes place just after a great battle between the army of the King of Scotland and a rebel Scottish army supported by the King of Norway.

Act I. Scene I

An open place.
Thunder and lightning. Enter three WITCHES

FIRST WITCH: When shall we three meet again
In thunder lightning or in rain?
SECOND WITCH: When the hurlyburly's done,
When the battle's lost and won.
THIRD WITCH: That will be ere the set of sun.
FIRST WITCH: Where the place?
SECOND WITCH: Upon the heath.
THIRD WITCH: There to meet with Macbeth.
FIRST WITCH: I come Graymalkin!
SECOND WITCH: Paddock calls.
THIRD WITCH: Anon!
ALL: Fair is foul, and foul is fair;
Hover through the fog and filthy air.
[Exeunt]

Scene II

A camp near Forres.
Alarum within. Enter DUNCAN, MALCOLM, DONALBAIN,
LENNOX, *with* ATTENDANTS, *at one door, and a bleeding*
CAPTAIN *at the other.*

DUNCAN: What bloody man is that? He can report,
As seemeth by his plight, of the revolt
The newest state.
MALCOLM: This is the sergeant
Who like a good and hardy soldier fought
'Gainst my captivity. Hail brave friend.
Say to the King the knowledge of the broil
As thou didst leave it.
CAPTAIN: Doubtful it stood,
As two spent swimmers, that do cling together
And choke their art. The merciless Macdonwald
Worthy to be a rebel, for to that
The multiplying villainies of nature
Do swarm upon him - from the Western Isles
Of kerns and gallowglasses is supplied,
And fortune on his damned quarrel smiling
Showed like a rebel's whore. But all's too weak,
For brave Macbeth - well he deserves that name -
Disdaining fortune, with his brandished steel,
Which smoked with bloody execution,
Like valour's minion carved out his passage,
Till he faced the slave;
Which ne'er shook hands, nor bade farewell to him,
Till he unseamed him from the nave to th' chops,
And fixed his head upon our battlements.

kerns and gallowglasses :
Irish soldiers
whore : prostitute
valour : courage
unseamed : unstitched

Activities

1 Look first at the first scene. Are there any words in this which you would not expect people to use today? If so, which are they and what do they mean ?

2 Now look at the second scene. Read it carefully and work out roughly what is being said. Who is the Captain and what is his message ?

3 Some of the words in this scene are probably unfamiliar to you. For example: **broil minion nave chops**. Can you work out from the context what each one means ?

4 Other words have changed their meaning since Shakespeare's time. For example: **spent steel**. What do you think each of these means in the scene ?

5 Can you see any differences between the grammar of this extract and modern English grammar ?

The 15th Century

During the Middle Ages, most drama was religious and told the stories of the Bible and the saints. At great religious occasions, some large cities used to have festivals , or 'cycles', of plays which told the stories of the Old and New Testaments. They were performed on makeshift mobile stages, called pageants. This extract comes from the beginning of *The Second Shepherds' Play*, which tells the story of how the shepherds heard the news of the birth of Jesus Christ.

(Scene: field near Bethlehem.)

(1)

I PASTOR: Lord, what these weders are cold! And I am yll happyd.

I am nere hand dold,   so long have I nappyd;

My legys thay fold,   my fyngers ar chappyd.

It is not as I wold,   for I am al lappyd

In sorow.

In stormes and tempest,

Now in the eest, now in the west,

Wo is hym has never rest

Myd day nor morow!

happyd: covered
nere hande, nere handys: near, nearby
dold: stupid
nappyd: slept
lappyd: entangled

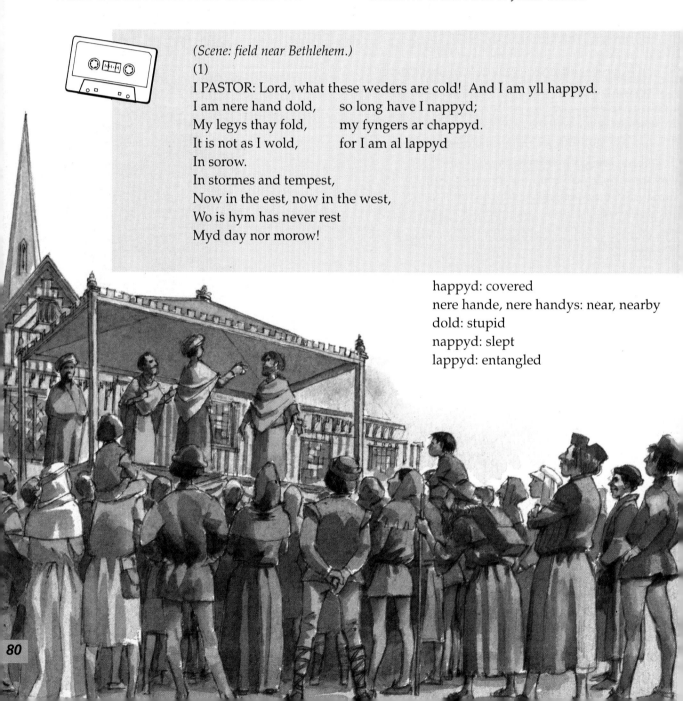

(2)

Bot we sely shepardes that walkys on the moore,
In fayth we are nere handys   outt of the doore.
No wonder, as it standys,   if we be poore,
For the tylthe of oure landys   lyys falow as the floore,
As ye ken.
We are so hamyd,
For-taxed and ramyd,
We are mayde hand tamyd
With thys gentlery men.

sely: simple
tylthe: tilth
lyys: lies
floore: floor
hamyd: hamstrung

For-taxed: over-taxed
ramyd: oppressed
hand tamyd: tame
gentlery men: gentry

Activities

1 Use the word list to help you work out what the speaker means.

2 Choose one of the two speeches and make up a modern English version. Don't worry about staying too close to the original speech - make it sound like real modern English speech.

3 Obviously a lot of the words have changed. Some have different spellings, while others have different meanings. Find examples of each kind of difference.

4 The grammar of sentences has changed, too. See if you can find examples of this.

Wha me mudder do

Mek me tell you wha me Mudder do
wha me mudder do
wha me mudder do

Me mudder pound plantain mek fufu
Me mudder catch crab mek calaloo stew

Mek me tell you wha me Mudder do
wha me mudder do
wha me mudder do

Me mudder beat hammer
Me mudder turn screw
She paint chair red
then she paint it blue

Mek me tell you wha me Mudder do
wha me mudder do
wha me mudder do

Me mudder chase bad-cow
with one 'Shoo'
she paddle down river
in she own canoe
Ain't have nothing
dat me mudder can't do

Ain't have nothing
dat me mudder can't do

Mek me tell you

Grace Nichols

Accent and dialect

Claire, Matthew and Tom read the poem and talked about it.

What is it about ?

Tom	It's about a negro child speaking about her mother - his -
Claire	There are three of them : it's as though she's got a family of three and they're all talking about their mother.
Matthew	It's it's either...we don't actually think that it's actually written by who it's supposed to - you know - portray. We think it's simulated to sound as if it's - you know - African or wherever it comes from.

Where does it come from ?

Tom	We're pretty sure that it's African...sort of thing...
John	Why African ?
Tom	Well it's...the way we hear Africans portrayed on television and in the media and stuff. It's -
Matthew	It's stereotyped.
Tom	Yes. It's...
John	What's 'stereotyped' ?
Matthew	Well it's a kind of - like - Irish are all - you know - a bit thick and then we portray Africans as a bit basic, if you see what I mean. And it's got that kind of rhythm of - you know - of the drums, if you see what I mean, that we associate with Africa.

What do you think ?

1 What do you think the poem is about ?

2 Where do you think it comes from, and why ?

3 Grace Nichols helps us 'hear' the poem as we read it, by the way she spells the words:

mudder for mother

wha for what

Try reading the poem aloud. What kind of accent does it make you use and where do you think it comes from ?

4 She also uses dialect words that are not part of Standard English. Make a list of them and try to work out from the poem what each one might mean.

Dialect grammar

The poem by Grace Nichols uses a dialect which differs from Standard English in three important ways:

- use of personal pronouns
- agreement of verbs
- use of the article

1 Read the poem again and find examples of each of these.

2 Study these examples and work out how the dialect differs from Standard English.

3 Write an explanation of what you have found out. The information on pages 84 and 85 will help you.

word classes

We can classify words according to the ways in which they are used in sentences. One class of words in English is called pronouns.

Personal pronouns

This is a complete table of all the personal pronouns in Standard English. Study it and see if you can work out why the pronouns have been arranged in the way that they have.

I	me	myself	my	mine
we	us	ourselves	our	ours
you	you	yourself	your	yours
you	you	yourselves	your	yours
he	him	himself	his	his
she	her	herself	her	hers
it	it	itself	its	
they	them	themselves	their	theirs

Standard or non-Standard ?

Some of these sentences use Standard English pronouns, and some use non-Standard. Which is which and why?

1 Give me me pencil back !

2 He should've done it hisself and not asked someone else to.

3 She done it herself.

4 That engine won't go because her's out of fuel. That's what.

Verbs and agreement

In Standard English the verb in a sentence has to agree with its subject.

	Subject	Verb	Rest of the sentence
Singular	She	loves	chocolate ice cream.
	My friend from Berwick		
Plural	They	hate	our noisy dogs.
	The boy down the road and the family next door		

Verb forms

For most verbs, the changes we have to make are very simple:

	Present	Past
I	hate	hated
we	hate	hated
you	hate	hated
she	hates	hated
he	hates	hated
it	hates	hated
they	hate	hated

For a small number of very important verbs the changes are more complicated. How would you fill in the gaps in this table ?

	Present	Past
I	am	was
we		
you		
she		
he		
it		
they		

Present	Past
do	

Present	Past
make	

How They Work

There was once a lad called Dauntless Little John, since he was afraid of nothing. Travelling about the world, he came to an inn, where he asked for lodgings.

lad	was	Dauntless	there
John	called	Little	once
world	travelling	afraid	
inn	came		
lodgings	asked		

a	whom	of	since
the	nothing	about	where
an	he	to	for

OPEN WORD CLASSES

These four classes continue to grow. The new words that are added to English are always members of these four classes. They are the 'bricks of meaning' which we use to build up sentences: *travelling world came inn asked lodgings*. (Notice that even though most of the words are there, it is still quite difficult to understand exactly what is meant.)

NOUNS

Nouns are a class of words referring to

people - lad

places - inn

things - world

ideas - happiness

ADJECTIVE

Adjectives are a class of words that work with nouns. Adjectives qualify nouns: they make their meaning clearer or fuller.

ADVERB

Adverbs are a class of words that work with verbs, adjectives or other adverbs. They modify these words: they make their meaning clearer or fuller.

She was running quickly. She's a really very fast runner.

They also do a number of other jobs:

There was once a lad called...

VERB

Verbs are a class of words that refer to actions or states. A sentence normally contains a verb.

CLOSED WORD CLASSES

These word classes are not growing. We use them like glue (or mortar) to join together the bricks of the open class words when we make up sentences: Travelling *about the* world *he* came *to an* inn *where he* asked *for* lodgings.

ARTICLE

Three words that work with nouns: *a, an, the*

PRONOUN

A class of words that generally work as a 'short cut' - they replace a noun or a noun phrase, and save time when we are speaking or writing: in the example, the word 'he' saves the writer having to say 'Dauntless Little John' every time.

PREPOSITION

Prepositions come before a noun or pronoun and link it to the rest of the sentence in some way.

CONJUNCTION

Conjunctions join two parts of the sentence together.

New words

1. Try to think of words you know that are new. They may be words for new inventions or discoveries, or they may be fashionable words that you and your friends use. Make a list of them.
2. For each one write a sentence in which it is used correctly. Put a circle round the word.
3. Against each word write down which word class it belongs to (as it is used in that sentence).

The sad story of the saggar bottom knocker

A saggar is a large pottery container inside which china is fired. This speaker from North Staffordshire describes what happened when he started work in a pottery and was given the job of knocking out saggar bottoms.

he'd got this er metal frame
and a lump of saggar marl and
he'd got this damn big mallet and
he started hammering away at it
and he says now that's all you got to do
knock them flat and that makes a saggar a
saggar a saggar bottom he says that's all you got
to do and you've got two frame makers here that
that make the side of the saggar and you've got
to keep them going with saggar bottoms well I
had a go at this I could feel blisters coming up on
me hands he came to me many a time and he
says look son you're holding that mallet wrong
you'll be doing yourself a more injury than good
he says you'll have to you'll have hit it hold it the
way that I showed you well I carried on and it
was oh it was killing me this this mallet it was

that damn big but I pressed on and then when
the the framemakers got a bit short and they
were waiting for bottoms one of them come
across and says look son try it like this and then
he'd show me again and knock couple out so's 'e
he could keep them going and er I kept going
well it jiggered me up he says well what you
going to what do you feel like I says oh I'm all
right yet I wouldn't give in I went back home at
the end of the shift and had me tea and looked at

me hands I'd got blisters as big as boils here coming on me hands so me mother says oh that job's too heavy for you son I says well I'll have to I says it I says I'll have to give it another go I won't I won't pack in after a day I'll give it another go so for cut a short er a long short story short I went the second day and during the afternoon m'hands are bleeding he came to me and he says look son he says I'm sorry I've got to stop thee thee't not cut out for this this job so he says if you like set down there he says and I'll get you your coppers what you've earned I'll pay you a fu- two full days pay he says although thee's got it's only about three o'clock now he says you've got a bit more to do he says but it's doing thee more harm than good so he paid me up and off I went back home

Dialect words

1 Read through the story and pick out any words that you would not normally expect to see in Standard English. Explain what they mean.

2 Now pick out any words that are used with a different meaning from the normal Standard English one. For each one explain what it means in Standard English and what it means in the story.

DIALECT GRAMMAR

This speaker uses a number of grammatical forms that are not Standard English. They are listed here. For each one explain what the Standard English form would be and what the grammatical difference is.

he says

me hands

it was that damn big

so's 'e could

he says

what you going to...

I...had me tea

...looked at me hands

me mother says

I says

so for cut

to stop thee

thee't not cut out

if you like set

your coppers what you've earned

thee's got

it's doing thee

STANDARD ENGLISH

Choose a section of about ten lines from the story. Look through the work you have done so far. Now make a written Standard English version of what the speaker said.

COUNTING
Sheep

Speaker: Well, it's something I've always been interested in, you know, I've been brought up with it. The first man that really introduced us to it was an old poet. He used to (write and) recite poetry and he knew all about these old Lakeland ways and I used to have a crack with him for night when I was going home from school and that's how I really got interested in it. He used to tell me all about the old ways all the old clipping days and the old counting.

Interviewer: Tell me some of those

Speaker: It goes back to the tally-stick days when sheep were counted by the score. They would count from one to twenty, put a notch on the tally-stick and then they would carry on again. And each valley had its own different dialect really...for counting.

Interviewer: Why ? What do you mean by that ?

Speaker: Well the area round here was : yan tyan tethera methera pimp sethera lethera othera dothera deek yandeek tyandeek tetheradeek metheradeek bumfit yanabumfit tyanabumfit tetherabumfit metherabumfit jiggit - and that was twenty you see and then a notch on the tally-stick and then another twenty.

Interviewer: Are there many of those old traditions still hanging around ?

Speaker: No, not now. I mean we still - words still come up that's in the Cumberland dialect such as we would say maybe, 'There's yaow sheep owwer thyere.'

Interviewer: And what would that mean if you would translate it ?

Speaker: Well that means 'There one.'

Cumbrian counting

1 Copy and complete this table:

2 Some of the words are repeated in the counting system. What is the pattern they follow ?

3 If you wanted to make up the words for the following numbers, what do you think they would be, and why ?
21 22 23 24 25

Number in figures	Standard English	Cumbrian dialect	Other English words I know for it
1	one		
2		tyan	
3			
20			score

Counting in French

Different languages use different systems for counting. This is because of the history of the language and of the people who used it in the past. Study the information in this table and then explain how the French counting system differs from the English one.

one	un	twelve	douze	thirty	trente
two	deux	thirteen	treize	fifty	cinquante
three	trois	fourteen	quatorze	sixty	soixante
four	quatre	fifteen	quinze	seventy	soixante-dix
five	cinq	sixteen	seize	seventy-one	soixante et onze
six	six	seventeen	dix-sept	seventy-five	soixante-quinze
seven	sept	eighteen	dix-huit	seventy-nine	soixante-dix-neuf
eight	huit	nineteen	dix-neuf	eighty	quatre-vingts
nine	neuf	twenty	vingt	ninety	quatre-vingt-dix
ten	dix	twenty-one	vingt et un	ninety-one	quatre-vingt-onze
eleven	onze	twenty-two	vingt-deux	ninety-eight	quatre-vingt-dix-huit

Telling the time in Kiswahili

Different languages have different ways of telling the time, too. The table below gives information about numbers in Kiswahili (a language spoken along the East Coast of Africa and in Kenya and Tanzania). It also tells you about telling the time. See if you can work out the system it uses.

one.................... moja
two.................... mbili
three................. tatu
four.................... nne
five.................... tano
six.................... sita
seven................ saba
eight................ nane
nine................... tisa
ten.................... kumi
eleven.............. kumi na moja
twelve.............. kumi na mbili
and so on to
twenty.............. ishirini

7 am...... seven o'clock........... saa moja
8 am...... eight o'clock........... saa mbili
noon...... twelve o'clock........ saa sita
3pm....... three o'clock.......... saa tisa
5pm....... five o'clock............. saa kumi na mbili

Questions

1 How would you say these numbers in French ?
73 78 84 89 95

2 How would you say these numbers in Kiswahili ?
14 17 19

3 How would you say these times in Kiswahili ?
9 am 11 am 2 pm 6 pm

It depends what you mean

Different languages don't just have different words. They actually divide things up in different ways.

WHAT COLOUR ?

If you had to choose one word to describe colour 'A', what would you choose ? And 'B' ? And 'C' ?

You may have chosen two or three different words. The most likely words in English are 'blue', 'green', and 'turquoise'. If you had been a Navaho from North America, you would have used the same word for all three. Navaho only has one word for all three.

The spectrum is continuous; it isn't divided into distinct separate colours. Different languages divide it in different ways. In this diagram, you can see the different ways in which English and literary Welsh (the language in which books used to be written in Wales) describe certain colours.

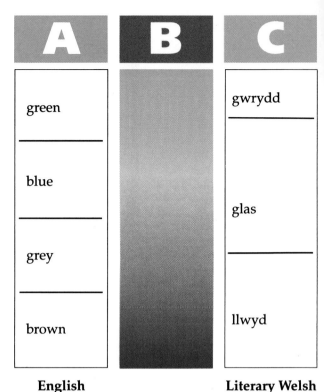

A	B	C
green		gwrydd
blue		glas
grey		
brown		llwyd

English   **Literary Welsh**

Family names

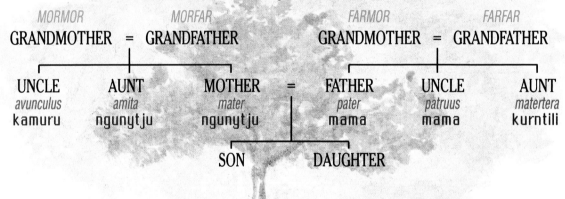

MORMOR	MORFAR		FARMOR		FARFAR
GRANDMOTHER	= GRANDFATHER		GRANDMOTHER	=	GRANDFATHER

UNCLE	AUNT	MOTHER	=	FATHER	UNCLE	AUNT
avunculus	amita	mater		pater	patruus	matertera
kamuru	ngunytju	ngunytju		mama	mama	kurntili

SON   DAUGHTER

Key

MORFAR	Swedish
avunculus	Latin
ngunytju	Pitjanjatjara

EXPLANATIONS, PLEASE

1 Study the diagram and the key.
2 Explain how these three languages differ from English in the way they describe the different members of the family.
3 By studying a language we can learn about the history and beliefs of the people who spoke that language in the past. What can you work out from these examples about how the speakers of these languages used to think about families and relationships ?

Be a language expert

Karkish, Glemp, and Kataga are three recently discovered languages. They seem to work in rather strange ways, and you have been asked to find out about their vocabulary. This page shows the names they give to a number of ordinary objects. See if you can work out what the words illustrated mean.

kliffos glarg sabata	*klimpa* glarg sabata	*kliffos* glimp sabata	
klimpa glimp sabata	*klimpa* glarg tapada	*klimpa* glimp tapada	
montu clat lamana	*moffos* clat lamana	*montu* clunger lamana	
montu clunger vabada	*montu* clunger lamana	*moffos* clat vabada	
tarka frasple zawaka	*tarka* frasple zawaka	*tarka* frasple sawaga	
sofka frasple sawaga	*sofka* frod sawaga	*tarka* frod sawaga	

Explanations

1 Work out what the words in the three languages mean.

2 Make up vocabulary lists like these:

Karkish	Glemp	Kataga
kliffos	glarg	tapada
klimpa	glimp	sabata
montu	clunger	lamana
moffos	clat	vabada
tarka	frasple	zawaka
sofka	frod	sawaga

Note: Answers are given at the end of the cassette.

summary

WHA ME MUDDER DO

Accent is the way in which a person pronounces the words of a language. People from different places or from different social groups often have different accents.

WORD CLASSES

We can divide words up according to the ways in which they can be used in sentences. The four open word classes are: nouns, verbs, adjectives and adverbs. These all contain words with a 'dictionary meaning', and new words are being added to them as the language develops. The four closed classes are: articles, pronouns, prepositions, and conjunctions. These contain a much smaller (and fixed) number of words which help with the construction of sentences. Two important ways in which dialects can differ grammatically from Standard English are in their use of personal pronouns and verbs.

THE SAD STORY OF THE SAGGAR BOTTOM KNOCKER

Both these grammatical differences are illustrated in this dialect story.

COUNTING SHEEP

Different dialects and languages have different counting systems and ways of telling the time. This often helps us to understand about the lives of the people who spoke those languages in the past.

IT DEPENDS WHAT YOU MEAN

Basic ideas like colour and family relationships are expressed in different ways by different languages - according to the needs and the experience of the people who spoke those languages in the past. When linguists study a new language, they have to forget about how their own language does things and try to work out how the new language expresses things.

Grammatical terms

Word	See page(s)	Explanation
adjective	85	A class of words that work with nouns. Adjectives qualify nouns - they make their meaning fuller or clearer.
adverb	85	A class of words that work with verbs, adjectives, and other adverbs to make their meaning clearer or fuller.
adverbial	40	The adverbial part of a sentence gives the answer to questions like: When ? Where ? How ? She threw it away. We are going to the pictures.
affix		Part of a word that comes before or after the stem.
article	85	The class of words that contains a, an, the.
aspect	41	The verb in a sentence has tense (see below) and aspect. The tense tells us about time, while the aspect gives us more information. There are three aspects in English: simple — I walk continuous — I am walking perfect — I have walked
command	40	see sentence types
complement	40	The complement comes after the verb in sentences like these: Peter seems very unhappy Mrs Weeks is our English teacher It is different from an object as you can see by comparing these two sentences: Mr Green met our postman. - SUBJECT+VERB+OBJECT Mr Green is our postman. - SUBJECT+VERB+COMPLEMENT
compound	69	A word that is made up of two existing words joined together. (eg birdcage)
conjunction	38, 85	Conjunctions join two parts of the sentence together. For example: and, but, as, if, when, because
exclamation	40	see sentence types
loan word	66	A word that is 'borrowed' from another language.
noun	84	A class of words referring to people, places, things, ideas.

Heinemann Educational
a division of Heinemann Educational Books Ltd
Halley Court, Jordan Hill, Oxford, OX2 8AZ.

OXFORD LONDON EDINBURGH
MELBOURNE SYDNEY AUCKLAND
IBADAN NAIROBI GABORONE HARARE
KINGSTON PORTSMOUTH NH(USA)
SINGAPORE MADRID BOLOGNA ATHENS

British Library Cataloguing In Publication Data
Seely, John
        Language Live!
        Bk.2
        1.Language
        I.Title
        400

        ISBN 0–435–10241–9

Designed and illustrated by
Plum Design, Southampton

Printed and bound in Spain
by Mateu Cromo

Acknowledgments

We should like to thank the following for their help in the production of this book:
Staff and children at The Chase School, Malvern, especially Robin Ancrum, Claire, Tom, Matthew, Becky and Katherine.
Kirsty Robson and Melanie Ashcroft, Community Service Volunteers (and Sylvia Lacey of CSV, Hereford & Worcester for setting things up), plus the staff and residents at the Orchard Street Centre, Kidderminster, and the staff and children of Westfield School, Leominster.

We would like to thank the following for permission to reproduce copyright material:
BBC for 'The Sad Story of the Saggar Bottom Knocker', 'Counting Sheep' and the text on p13; *Blitz* Magazine for cover and pages from *Blitz*, March 1990; Butler, Borg, Millets, Fraser LRC Ltd for Moroccan brochure; Churchman Publishing Ltd for extract from *The Holy Gospel of John* by Peter Levi; Consumer's Association for 'Your Views on Green products' from *Which?*, September 1989; *Elle* magazine and Angel Holden for 'Julia Roberts and Carre Otis' article from *Elle*, March 1990; Editions Gautley for *Plan Guide to Tangier*, Editions Gautley 1979; Methuen, a division of the Octopus Publishing Group for extract from 'Find Me' from the *The Bankrupt and Other Plays* by David Mercer; National Television Records Office for Television Licence; Grace Nichols for 'Wha me Mudder Do' from *Black Poetry*, ed. Grace Nichols, Blackie 1988; Random House Ltd for extract from *Midnight Mass and Other Stories* by Paul Bowles, Arena 1986 and for extract from *Tangier, A Writer's Notebook* by Angus Stewart, Hutchinson 1977; *Smash Hits* for cover and pages from *Smash Hits* February 1990; Thomson Tour Operators for 'Morocco, Tangier' from *Thomson Summer Sun* brochure; Transworld for cover and pages from *Elle*, March 1990; *Vanity Fair* for 'Pacino' article from *Elle*, March 1990;

Although every effort has been made to contact copyright holders before publication it has not always been possible. We would be pleased to rectify any omissions at the first opportunity.

We would like to thank the following for permission to reproduce photographs on the pages noted:

Barnaby's Picture Library p63 right; BBC p13; BBC/Syndication International p47; Gladstone Pottery Museum pp86-7; Sally & Richard Greenhill Ltd p16; Karin Model Agency for photograph of Yasmeen on Elle March 1990 cover p25; Bridgit Lacombe p30; The Mansell Collection p63 left; Mary Evans Picture Library p62, p76; Patrick Sutherland p36; Chris Ridgers pp5-10; John Seely pp36,43,49-55; Lance Staedle p30; South American Pictures/Tony Morrison p46.